RADIO CONTROLLED HELICOPTERS

The guide to building and flying R/C helicopters

RADIO CONTROLLED HELICOPTERS

The guide to building and flying R/C helicopters

Nick Papillon

SPECIAL INTEREST MODEL BOOKS

Special Interest Model Books Ltd.
Stanley House
3 Fleets Lane
Poole
Dorset
BH15 3AJ

First published by Nexus Special Interests Ltd. 1996

This edition published by S.I.Model Books Ltd. 2003
Reprinted 2004

ISBN 1-85486-226-X

Contents

CHAPTER 1

Introduction

I have spent many enjoyable hours building and flying radio controlled helicopters over the last twenty years and I am in absolutely no doubt that it is one of the most fascinating and rewarding of hobbies.

While most people reading this book will be doing so because they have decided to take up the hobby, some of you may still be uncertain. I hope that you will join the growing number of helicopter fliers and the first aim of this book is to provide you with the information which you will need to decide whether flying a radio controlled helicopter is what you want to do.

The second aim is to try to provide you with all the information which you will need to progress safely from novice to competent pilot, with a minimum of difficulty and expense.

Some of you will already be flying fixed-wing models and you will find that much of what you know will be of use. However, flying helicopters is very different and experience of flying fixed-wing models can be both a help and, occasionally, a hindrance.

Radio controlled helicopters are comparatively new within the aeromodelling scene. It was not until 1967 that a serious attempt was made to solve the problems of scaling down a flying machine whose aerodynamics are immensely complex and, even now, not fully understood. In 1970, Dieter Schlüter set a world endurance record of 27 minutes 51 seconds and a closed circuit distance record of 11.5 kilometres. Twenty-five years on, the English Channel has been crossed and boredom is probably the chief factor which limits endurance records.

There is one popular myth which I should dispel and that is that you should take up flying helicopters, rather than fixed-wing models, because you can fly them in your back garden. Well, I don't know how big your back garden is but when you are learning to fly a helicopter, no space is too large. You need just as large an area for flying helicopters as you do for flying fixed-wing

Figure 1.1 *Then and now – the Schlüter Cobra was the first scale kit to be available and this photograph was taken in 1973. The Hiroba Lama (below) appeared twenty years later.*

Figure 1.2 *The Hiroba Lama.*

models, even if you don't actually use all of it.

Finally, and most importantly, radio controlled helicopters are not toys. Even the smaller helicopters weigh about 3 kg and fly at up to sixty miles an hour, while the tips of the main rotor blades are travelling at up to four hundred miles an hour and are potentially lethal. Always remember the damage which the model can do and never take chances, whether you are flying or just intending to run the engine on the ground.

Please note; all references throughout this book are to models weighing up to 7 kg without fuel. A typical pod and boom model powered by a .60 cu.in. engine will weigh about 5 kg. If you wish to fly a model weighing more than 7 kg, you should contact the BMFA for details of the requirements

The objectives of the book

This book has been written with the intention of guiding the complete novice through the mysteries of buying, building and flying his first radio controlled helicopter. I have tried to cover all aspects of the process in sufficient depth for someone who has no previous knowledge, either of radio control or of flying models, to be able to succeed in this aim. Inevitably this means that some subjects may seem to be laboured, particularly if you have some prior knowledge of the hobby or are already an experienced fixed-wing flier, but please do read all the sections, albeit briefly, because helicopters really are different.

For a first helicopter, I am convinced that only the pod and boom type is suitable as a training machine and that you should start with a 30-size model. I have assumed throughout the book that this is the type of model which you will be flying, although a short chapter is included on scale models.

A brief review of the chapters

Chapter 2. The advantages of flying helicopters

Fixed wing versus rotary – just what are the advantages of flying helicopters as opposed to fixed wing models?

Chapter 3. Where do I begin?

You have decided to give helicopters a try, so what next? All the things you will need to consider, including finding and joining a club, flying sites, models, engines, radios, insurance and so on.

Chapter 4. Choosing the model

Kit or ARTF, basic or GT; helicopters can be bought either as kits or as almost-ready-to-fly (ARTF) models – which is the better? What about a scale model? Or an electric one? Or a second-hand one?

Chapter 5. All about engines

The engine: how it works, how to adjust it and what it needs, including mufflers, glow plugs and fuel.

Chapter 6. Everything you need to know about radio systems

What you need, how it works, why helicopter radios are different and what they do, and gyros.

Chapter 7. All about rotor blades

Tells you how to assemble wooden blades and how to cover and balance all kinds, and how to make your own balancer.

Chapter 8. Finding your own flying site

If you haven't found a club to join, all the aspects you will need to consider for your own flying site.

Chapter 9. Accessories and training aids

The accessories you need for flying the model and the others which could be helpful, including training undercarriages, buddy boxes and simulators.

Chapter 10. Building the model

What you need and how to do it, including installing the engine, fuel system and radio.

Chapter 11. Installing the radio

What the transmitter functions do and how to install and connect the radio in the model.

Chapter 12. Setting up the model

What you are trying to achieve, why and how to do it, including adjusting the gyro.

Chapter 13. Before your first flight

Getting everything ready.

Chapter 14. The day arrives

The weather is fine, your instructor is available, everything is ready . . .

Chapter 15. Hovering, circuits and simple aerobatics

Basic flying techniques – what comes next.

Chapter 16. Routine maintenance

Don't just chuck it in the corner when you get home (with a few tips on troubleshooting on the flying field).

Chapter 17. After the crash

They do happen but they're rarely terminal – what to look for and how to fix it.

Chapter 18. Scale models

Kit, conversion or scratch-built.

Chapter 19. Conclusions and useful addresses

CHAPTER 2

The advantages of flying helicopters

Fixed wing versus rotary – why helicopters are better

Helicopters are different, that much is plain to see, but why should you decide you want to fly one? There are many differences between rotary- and fixed-wing models, apart from the obvious ones. Incidentally, both fixed- and rotary-wing models are aircraft. We call rotary-wing aircraft 'helicopters' but there seems to be no satisfactory alternative to the somewhat clumsy term 'fixed wing' when it is necessary to distinguish between the two.

Choosing your model

Fixed wing

When you start to fly, you will need to buy a suitable trainer. It is virtually impossible to learn to fly using the sort of aerobatic or scale machine to which you will want to progress when you are competent, so you will have to have at least two models. If you are going to fly large models, you will need a large engine, and, as this will be unsuitable for your trainer, you will also need two engines.

Helicopters

Helicopters do not come in a wide variety of shapes or sizes. They are generally classified by their engine sizes and are referred to as 'thirty' or 'sixty' machines, the former group being powered by engines of between 0.32 cu.in. and 0.36 cu.in. capacity and the latter group being powered by engines of 0.61 cu.in. capacity. There are a small number of 0.46 cu.in. powered machines of which the Morley Maverick is the best known.

Most people starting with helicopters do so with a thirty size machine. However, so versatile are these models that many of them remain with this size and never feel the urge to fly one of the larger helicopters. There is no such thing as a trainer helicopter – it is simply a matter of how the machine is set up, as you will see. The helicopter which is set up to be stable and easy to handle can perform aerobatics literally at the flick of a switch on the transmitter.

Building your model . . .

Fixed wing

These are built either from a plan or from a kit and the skills involved include transferring the drawings to the materials, cutting out the components, assembling and gluing, then covering and painting the finished model. The finished models come in a wide variety of shapes and sizes.

Scale models are common and not particularly demanding to build, particularly if you start with a kit, although the amount of detail which may be added is almost limitless.

Fixed-wing modellers often tend to be either builders or fliers, and the builders of the most detailed scale models often seem to be much more interested in the building than in the flying!

Helicopters

A helicopter is always built from a kit. You may buy the machine either in component form or almost completely pre-assembled, but you will not have to do any shaping or gluing or covering or painting, unless you decide to build a scale model. Building a helicopter consists of screwing or bolting together a large number of metal and plastic components, with an instruction book and diagrams to guide you. The tools involved can be as few as two or three spanners and two or three Allen keys, the only other requirement being a flat surface which, ideally, can be wiped clean.

Scale helicopters are very much the exception, most models being of what is called the 'pod and boom' configuration. There are only a few scale kits available and they are more expensive than pod and boom models. Apart from painting the canopy if you want to, there is little need or opportunity for self-expression!

Almost all helicopter pilots are fliers first and foremost, although whether this is due to the lack of scale opportunities or the nature of the people who are interested in mechanical devices, I would not care to speculate.

. . . and flying it

Fixed-wing models

When you have built your model, you will need to find someone to teach you to fly it and this will involve starting from high in the sky and working downwards. This means that you will go out to the flying field where your instructor will take your model off, climb it to a safe height and then give the transmitter to you so that you can discover the effect of the controls. After about ten minutes he will resume control so that he can land the model for refuelling.

Progress is measured by the diminishing frequency with which the instructor prises the transmitter from your clutches between each take-off and landing. You will gradually fly lower and lower, deliberately as opposed to accidentally, until eventually you will be able to do your own take-offs and landings. Only then will you be able to fly unassisted and when you choose.

Any crash at this stage is likely to damage the model and, while repairs may not be expensive, they can be very time-consuming. This is a big deterrent when all you want to do is to get on with learning to fly.

Helicopters

Helicopters are different. You start from the ground and work upwards and you can even do it alone (although I don't recommend it at first). You will need someone to set your model up – the Catch-22 of helicopters is that they won't fly unless they have been set up and you can only set them up by flying them. However, once the model has been flown and you have been given a demonstration of the effect of the controls, it is all down (or up) to you. You can go out on your own and teach yourself, starting by opening the throttle until the model is just light enough on its skids to slide around. You can observe the response to the various controls and you can gradually build up instinctive reactions to the model's antics.

The major differences are that you learn at your own pace, you fly as often as you like and there is little pressure on you to fly when the weather is unsuitable, just because that is the only day when your instructor is available. If you have the patience to practise and you do not try to progress too fast, there is no reason why you should damage the model while you are learning. If you do tip the model over and damage something, the repairs are usually simple and you can easily be flying again the next day.

Transport and storage

The average fixed-wing model in the club to which I belong has a wingspan of about fifty-five inches and it has to be dismantled in order to fit in a car. My thirty size helicopter is forty-two inches in length with the main blades folded and it can be carried using just two fingers of one hand. It fits easily into the boot of most small cars and stands on a shelf when it is at home.

Furthermore, there are none of the problems of fixed-wing models where you need to protect the covering of the wing and fuselage from sharp objects. Helicopters are much less at risk from the small knocks and scratches which all fixed-wing models seem to suffer in transport and storage – accurately referred to as 'hangar rash' by fixed-wing fliers.

Helicopters are cleaner than fixed-wing models. The exhaust residue is blown downwards and does not cover the side of the fuselage as it does with fixed-wing models. All that is required when you arrive home is to wipe off any mud on the skids and to stand the model somewhere so that any oil which may drip from the exhaust outlet will not cause a problem. The alternative is to push a small piece of rag or kitchen towel into the exhaust outlet but you will then need to remember to remove it before trying to start the engine when next you go flying.

Maintenance

As with any machinery, routine maintenance is required with a helicopter but this only consists of checking that everything is still tight and showing no signs of wear. The advantage with a helicopter is that you can see all the components and it is a quick job to inspect everything when putting the model away. Although it is always a good idea to check, there are few problems with nuts and bolts working loose if you take all the usual precautions when assembling the model, as I will describe in Chapter 10.

The relative costs

There is no doubt that it costs more to start from scratch with a helicopter than it does with a fixed-wing model – at the time of writing, we tell anyone who joins our club that it will cost them about two to two and a half times as much. This is not only because of the higher cost of the model but also because you cannot use the cheapest radio and you will need to buy a starter and twelve volt battery in addition to any other basic equipment. However, if you are already flying fixed-wing models, you may already own these additional items.

Once you are a competent flier, helicopters can be cheaper than fixed-wing models because one model can be set up to fly in different ways and can be adjusted to suit your requirements. Moreover, if you decide that you want to fly a scale model, you may be able simply to fit a fuselage to your existing machine.

CHAPTER 3

Where do I begin?

You have decided to give helicopters a try, so what next?

Despite the undoubted popularity of model flying in the UK, when you want some advice, just like policemen, there's never anyone around to ask. The objective of this chapter is to summarise the various aspects of model flying to which you will need to give consideration – in some cases before you actually buy the model.

The obvious requirements are a helicopter and engine, and a radio control system. Equally obvious, but something which many potential modellers seem to take for granted, is somewhere to fly the model and finding this should really be your first priority. The best place to start, and a potential source of advice about everything which you will need, is your local model club.

The model club

How to find one

There are currently about five hundred clubs which are affiliated to the British Model Flying Association (and an unknown number which are not) so there should be a club within a reasonable distance of you. Not all of them will have a helicopter section but, if you find one which hasn't, they may still be able to tell you of another club which has, or you may be able to join and start one. The nearest club is usually fairly easy to find and the best starting point is the local model shop or, failing that, try telephoning other model shops in the area. You can often find details of model shops from their advertisements in the modelling magazines.

The BMFA has details of all the affiliated clubs and will give you the address and phone number of the club contact. The Model Pilots Association may also be able to help.

The local library may have details of any clubs on its database – aeromodelling is a recognised sport. You may possibly find details on a noticeboard in the library.

If none of these produces any information, you can try the modelling magazines. They sometimes have details of clubs but only if the clubs have sent them in (and kept them up to date).

Joining the club and what it will provide

When you do discover how to contact the membership secretary, don't waste time but do it immediately. Unfortunately, many clubs, particularly in the south of England, are oversubscribed and have waiting lists. The best time to join is just after the New Year, when most clubs will have had a few members who have decided not to renew their memberships, but you should never delay in putting your name on the waiting list. If there is a choice of clubs, put your name on the waiting lists for all of them, no matter how hopeless it may seem. Even if everyone renews their memberships, it is not uncommon for a club to decide to increase the total number of members, thereby creating unexpected vacancies.

Even if you cannot actually join and fly immediately, many clubs will allow you to turn up at the flying field to watch and to talk to members. This can be a good opportunity to get help and advice, to see which models and radios are popular, and to find someone who can teach you to fly when you join. Furthermore, you may be able to go ahead with buying and building your model while you are waiting to join and, if you do finish the model, you may well be able to find someone who will set it up for you and test fly it. This will all save time when you are able to start flying yourself.

The most important thing which you will have found when you join a club is somewhere to fly. If there are other helicopter fliers in the club, you will also have discovered a source of advice and support for those moments when it all seems to be going wrong and you are making no progress at all. The club will have an insurance scheme, providing third party cover for several million pounds, and there will probably be regular meetings and some sort of social activity – usually centring on the local pub!

I cannot recommend too strongly that you should join a club if you have the chance. It will remove many of the difficulties which you will otherwise encounter if you try to go it alone.

The helicopter and engine

Both these items are covered in detail in their own sections later in the book but there are a few points which are worth considering at this stage.

Another advantage of joining a club is that you will be able to see which models are popular. This will not only be an indication of which ones are reliable but also of the availability of spares and support from the local model shop, although the increasing popularity of mail order makes this less important than it used to be.

If you cannot join a club, you will have to be guided by the advice of the model shop from which you eventually buy the model. If you visit a model shop, make sure that whoever you are talking to actually knows about helicopters and flies them. Occasionally you may find the odd helicopter kit or second-hand machine for sale in a shop which does not normally sell helicopters, and these are best avoided. Before you decide to buy, ask the shop if they can provide a setting-up service afterwards and what sort of spares they have in stock. If the shop cannot set the helicopter up for you when you have built it (and you don't know anyone else who can), then I recommend that you look elsewhere. As you will see in the later chapters, it is virtually impossible to build and fly a helicopter unless you have some help from a competent flier and I would strongly advise you not even to consider trying, even if you have considerable fixed-wing experience.

Radio equipment

Again, this is covered in depth in its own section (Chapter 6). If you join a club, you will be able to see which makes are popular, although, in reality, there is little to choose from the point of view of reliability. You will be able to see which control mode is favoured and, if you can find someone who will be able to help you later, you will be able to consider the possibility of using a buddy box – this is covered in detail in Chapter 6.

If you are being advised by a model shop, go to the one which is selling you the helicopter, and the same comments as I have made about helicopter specialists also apply. Most model shops sell radio equipment but fixed-wing radio is not really suitable for flying helicopters.

You will need a gyro, which is also dealt with in Chapter 6.

Flying sites

Unfortunately, it can be all too difficult to find somewhere to fly, particularly in the south of England. While, at least in theory, you may fly a radio controlled model on any public land unless it is specifically banned, in practice model flying is usually specifically banned or restricted at public sites. The club of which I am a member recently used Ordnance Survey maps to draw one-mile radius circles (maximum radio range) anywhere where we would be 500 metres from houses (minimum noise separation). We discovered only two potential flying sites within about fifteen miles of our base – we were already using one of them and our neighbouring club was using the other!

Once again, joining a club is your best way of finding somewhere to fly. If that is impossible, you should read Chapter 8, *Finding your own flying site* which will give you an idea of what you will need to look for.

Insurance

There is no legal requirement for third party insurance but it is extremely foolish not to have it. There are several ways of obtaining insurance, but relying on your household policy is definitely not one of them.

By far the easiest way of obtaining insurance is to join one of the modelling organisations (whose addresses you will find at the end of the book). The British Model Flying Association is the governing body for model flying in the UK and membership of the BMFA automatically includes third party cover. The Model Pilots Association also offers insurance as an optional extra. The cover with both of these insurance policies is £5M in 1996. The third alternative is a specialist model flying insurance policy from an insurance broker but unless you know which policy to ask for (and I only know of one), you will be much better off if you go to one of the modelling organisations. The premium is typically about £6.00 for £5M, although the BMFA insurance is included in the membership fee.

If you join a model club, it will have arranged for insurance and the premium will be included in the membership fee.

CHAPTER 4

Choosing the model

Kit or ARTF, basic or GT; helicopters can be bought either as kits or as almost-ready-to-fly models – which is the better? What about a scale model? Or an electric one? Or a second-hand one?

The first thing which I should explain is that, unlike fixed-wing models, there is no such machine as a trainer helicopter. It is just that some helicopters are unsuitable for use as trainers and that includes scale models and 60-size machines, as well as helicopters which are not fitted with collective pitch (no matter how cheap they may seem).

Collective or fixed pitch

Fixed-pitch (or non-collective) helicopters have a pair of main rotor blades which are mounted on a hub which can pivot and this pivoting action allows you to control the direction in which the helicopter moves. The pitch of the main blades is fixed and the amount of lift is controlled by speeding up or slowing down the main blades, using the throttle.

Collective-pitch helicopters have a pair of main blades whose pitch may be altered individually to control the direction of the helicopter, or collectively to control the amount of lift. The throttle is linked to the collective pitch so that more power is applied when the pitch is increased, and vice versa, and the main rotor speed should never change while the helicopter is in flight.

Non-collective helicopters are more difficult to fly. This is particularly so in a wind, when control may be marginal during the descent because the main rotor speed has been reduced. The overwhelming preference for collective machines has meant that their price has come down to the point where the disadvantages of non-collective machines far outweigh any cost savings. Indeed, by the time you read this, the popularity of collective machines may have resulted in the complete disappearance of the non-collective versions.

Scale or pod and boom?

What on earth is a pod and boom model? The simplest answer is that it isn't a scale model – the name comes from the shape, where the canopy which covers most of the mechanics and radio installation is called the pod and the bit which sticks out of it and supports the tail is the boom. Probably more than 95 per cent of the helicopters sold are of this layout.

Figure 4.1 *The Morley Maverick and the TSK My Star (below) are typical pod and boom models which are built from kits.*

Figure 4.2 *The TSK My Star.*

You may have seen a scale model helicopter being flown and decided that you would like to fly a similar machine. Scale models can be bought as complete kits in the same way as pod and boom models but they are not suitable for training. The scale components are invariably more expensive than the simple canopy and fins of the pod and boom machines and they are also much more prone to damage. The mechanical components are less accessible, particularly where a fuselage is fitted, and the models are always more complex to build and repair. Finally, the extra weight of a scale model reduces the performance and makes flying it more difficult and demanding.

Thirty or sixty? Or electric?

Internal combustion (I/C) engines

'Thirty or sixty' of course refers to the engine size, as I explained in Chapter 2. While the larger machines which use the .60 cu.in. class of engine may be slightly easier to fly because the extra weight makes them a bit more stable, this advantage is largely offset by the slower response of the model to the controls. Furthermore they are *much* more expensive both to buy and to repair, with the spares and the engine costing as much as 50 per cent more than those for the smaller machines. The greater visibility of the larger helicopters is not a major help because you do not fly anything like as far away from yourself as you do with a fixed-wing trainer.

The current 30-46 class helicopters make ideal training machines and it is quite possible to fly the same model from learning the basic handling right through to aerobatics. You can even fit a scale fuselage later on if you want to.

Electric power

You may be tempted by the advantages of electric power. It is quiet and clean and you don't seem to need as many accessories. Unfortunately, all the advantages are totally offset by the poor endurance and the poor performance, which result from the low power-to-weight ratio of the motor/battery combination. The endurance will typically be around five minutes, whereas a tank of fuel will last around fifteen minutes. The recharging time will be about twenty minutes and you will either need to carry a small car battery for recharging, or you will need to return to your car (you can have a spare power pack but these cost £20 or more and changing them over takes longer than refuelling a conventional machine). The cost saving is largely illusory because of the need for micro servos, a speed controller and a battery charger for the power pack. The biggest disadvantage of electric helicopters, however, is the consequence of trying to maximise the poor performance – they are very lightly built, which makes them very fragile and therefore totally unsuitable as trainers. As you will discover, poor performance makes a helicopter significantly harder to fly, particularly in any wind.

I have flown a large electric helicopter but it used thirty-two nicad cells, so each power pack cost nearly £100, and the special charger, which was required to charge the 38.4V pack from a 12V car battery, cost more than a basic helicopter kit. The endurance was still only five minutes and the performance was much worse than the equivalent I/C powered machine.

Are they really the same?

When you decide the time has come to buy your first helicopter, you may well have to choose between a kit and an almost-ready-to-fly version of the same model. Furthermore, the ARTF version may also have the engine already installed.

The questions you really need to ask are what the finished model will have cost you and what its specification will be. If you look closely at the specifications of the models on offer, you will probably find that they are not the same, although the selling prices may not accurately reflect the differences in the finished machines. You will need to weigh up the advantages (and disadvantages) of having the model built for you (ARTF) as opposed to building it yourself but you will also need to know the specification of the finished model – this will give you some idea of the saving to be made if you can build the model yourself.

A manufacturer may produce up to three versions of the same basic design, all of them using the same size of engine. Furthermore, each version may be available either as a kit or as an ARTF model, and with or without an engine, although in general, kits do not include engines. All the versions will appear superficially similar and will share the same major components, such as side frames.

There may be differences in the colour scheme and decals, although we have so far been spared the equivalent of the company car drivers' obsessions with *GT*, *16V* and *turbo* and, unlike BMWs, you won't be charged extra for leaving the decals out!

Basic, sports or GT

The basic version of the helicopter will probably be fitted with ballraces where necessary for the mechanical components of the driving system. However, the control linkages will operate in plain bushes. The clutch may well use plastic shoes and a pressed steel bell.

The intermediate version may have ballraces in the control linkages and possibly other improvements such as metal clutch shoes.

The top specification version will be ballraced throughout and will have such extras as a machined clutch bell, metal clutch shoes and so on. Top start, where the engine is started by engaging a hexagonal shaft in a socket, may be fitted (belt start is the alternative, where the starter is held inside a flexible belt which is then pulled tight). Another starting method uses a rear cone, against which the starter is pressed before being operated, but models which use this method do not usually have alternative options (although the cone may be plastic on the cheaper version and aluminium on the more expensive one).

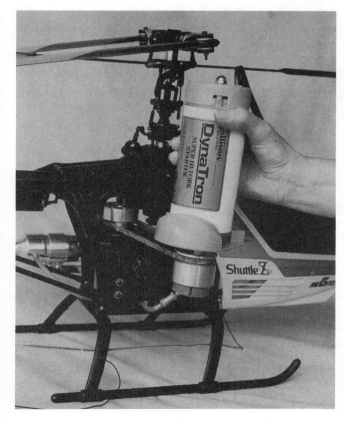

Figure 4.3 *This is a typical belt start system – the starter is pulled outwards to tighten the belt.*

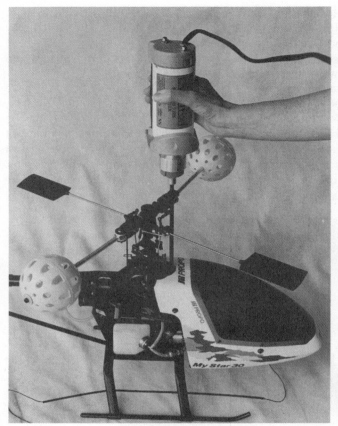

Figure 4.4 *A top start system uses a shaft with a hexagonal ball on the end.*

Kit or ARTF

An almost-ready-to-fly (ARTF) helicopter will require the installation of the radio equipment and possibly the engine. It will probably also require you to fit the undercarriage and to fit the main rotor to the top of the mast. The control linkages will require some adjustment but otherwise the machine will be ready to fly. However, there should be an instruction manual which gives all the information for completely disassembling and reassembling the model.

A kit will be just what it says. The main rotor head may be assembled but, apart from that, it will be a collection of numbered polythene bags, the contents of each of which will make up into a sub-assembly. The sub-assemblies will then be joined to finish the helicopter, the radio and engine being installed

Figure 4.5 *The socket in which the ball is engaged – a shaft and one-way bearing in the centre of the clutch shoes connect the socket to the flywheel.*

at some appropriate stage along the way. There will be an instruction manual which will take you through all the various assembly stages.

There are advantages and disadvantages to both. If you buy an ARTF model you save the time and effort involved in building. However, there may still be a fair amount of work involved before the model is ready to fly – particularly if the engine has not been installed – and you should also check that the manufacturer has not left any nuts or screws loose. Also, you will not have had the experience of building the model, which will stand you in good stead when you have to dismantle it for maintenance and repairs.

If you build the model from a kit, you will have a good understanding of how the various mechanical bits operate and where all the nuts and bolts are which may need to be tightened periodically. You will also probably have saved some money by buying a kit, or alternatively, you may have bought a higher specification version for the same price.

If it is a simple choice, I would recommend that you build the model from a kit. Most people who fly helicopters enjoy this type of creative work and the skills involved are fairly basic, with modern instruction manuals taking you through everything in easy stages. No more tools will be required than you will need for the subsequent maintenance and repair of the helicopter and the knowledge gained will save you time when you work on the machine in the future.

With or without an engine

It is often cheaper to have the engine included as part of the package, if you can still have the model specification which you require. Don't buy the wrong helicopter just because it offers a saving on the engine – ask the model shop if they will give you a discount if you buy the kit you want and an engine at the same time.

Where the engine is included with the helicopter by the kit manufacturer, there should be no problem if you subsequently want to remove the engine and install it in another helicopter of a different type. In general, particularly with 30-class helicopters, all engines currently fit all models (incidentally, this may well **not** be the case with the larger engine sizes of .46 cu.in. and upwards). It is worth asking in case this may change in the future.

So which one should you buy?

There is no need to buy the most expensive helicopter on the market unless you are absolutely convinced that you will still be flying it in several years' time. The basic version of a machine will fly just as well as the top specification one and it will go on doing it for long enough for you to become a competent flier.

If you are going it alone and you have absolutely no one from whom to seek help, then it does not matter too much which helicopter you buy, although the availability of spares should be a consideration. You should also try to compare the relative cost of spares for the various makes of helicopter, because there can be significant differences. If you have joined a club or have found someone to help you, then you can be guided by them because they will be familiar with the available choices.

From the point of view of the maintenance, the main difference between the basic version of a helicopter and the top specification one will be the length of time it takes for the bushes and clutch to wear out. You will be unable to tell the versions apart when you are flying them. The bushes will take many hours of flying before they show any visible signs of wear and will probably last a couple of years unless you start doing a lot of aerobatics. Plastic clutch shoes do wear, particularly when you start practising autorotations, but you may be able to upgrade to the metal ones when the plastic ones give up. Top starts are more convenient than belt starts and you don't have a belt to break, but they are expensive. Machined clutch bells, as opposed to pressed steel ones, last longer and, like metal clutch shoes, stand up better to those practice autorotations.

It may be possible to upgrade the basic machine in stages, but this is invariably more expensive than buying the higher specification to start with. If, however, you don't want all the extras which the top specification offers, it may pay you to buy the cheaper option and just fit the upgrade bits you want when the originals wear out.

Buying second-hand

You may find a second-hand helicopter in a model shop and you will see advertisements for helicopters for sale in the modelling magazines. Are they worth considering? Everything which follows applies equally whether the model is in a shop or is a private sale, because model shops often do not own the second-hand models which they sell — they are merely acting as agents for the private owners.

Before going to look at a model, ring up and find out exactly what is being included in the sale (rotor blades, radio, engine, gyro etc.) and the precise specification and age of each part, then find out the current retail price for what is on offer — new servos can range in price from about £15 to £100 (each, and there are five of them in a helicopter) and gyros vary from about £60 to £300. When you are deciding how much to pay, bear in mind that a model shop would probably give you a discount if you bought everything new, particularly if you bought it all at the same time.

If you are new to helicopters, ask someone who is experienced, and preferably familiar with the actual model being sold, to go and look at it with you. You should insist on seeing the model being flown — this is the only way in which you can be reasonably sure that it is complete and undamaged. Make sure that you will receive the model exactly as it is flown, not, for instance, with different main blades, and that the instructions are being included. Check also that the model you see being flown is exactly as you were told on the phone — once you have paid up and taken the model, it will probably be impossible to rectify any misunderstandings.

You should check that the seller is entitled to sell the model – unfortunately, models are stolen every year and they may be sold second-hand.

Finally, you will have missed the experience of building the model. This can make it more difficult to appreciate the workings of the helicopter when it is necessary to adjust and maintain it.

Bargains are definitely available in the second-hand market and the vast majority of sellers are honest, but there is no substitute for experience when buying anything which isn't new, and radio controlled helicopters are no exception.

CHAPTER 5

All about engines

The engine: how it works, how to adjust it and what it needs, including mufflers, glow plugs and fuel

Helicopter and fixed-wing engines, and recoil starters

When you compare the helicopter version of an engine with its fixed-wing equivalent, the main distinguishing feature is the cylinder head. The helicopter engine will have a much larger cooling area because of the relative lack of airflow around the head when the engine is running in a helicopter. This is the reason why you should always use the helicopter version of the engine, not the fixed-wing one.

There may be other differences but the only other one which you will be likely to notice is an extended throttle arm on the carburettor. The engine identification will often contain the letter H, as in '32H' or 'SX-H'.

There are two alternative versions of helicopter engines which you may see, those equipped with recoil starters and those equipped with rear cone starters. These engines are identical in all other respects but they do cost more than the standard versions.

Figure 5.1 *The OS 32 SX-H is a typical helicopter engine – note the large cooling fins. The glow plug and prop driver have been removed. The throttle arm is at the top and the throttle can be seen half open. The lower adjustment screw is the main needle valve.*

Recoil starters

You may be offered the choice of installing an engine which is equipped with a recoil starter – these have a small pull-start unit on the rear of the engine and they are started as you would a lawn mower.

Recoil starters can be a mixed blessing if you are not familiar with the handling of small two-stroke engines. While the engines do cost more than the conventional versions, they save the outlay on a starter and battery and you can arrive at the flying field with just a supply of fuel and a glow battery. However, the carburettor must be correctly adjusted for the starter to work successfully and recoil starters can be very tedious if the engine does not start fairly rapidly.

You will also need to check that the engine will fit the helicopter and whether any modifications will be necessary. If any changes to the model are required, it is worth considering what their effect may be – the installation in one model requires you to move the rear undercarriage cross member backwards by fitting an aluminium extension plate. Unfortunately, this plate now takes all the landing loads and is easily bent, which means that the model becomes unsuitable for use as a trainer.

Rear cone starters

This type of engine has the plain back plate replaced by one fitted with an aluminium cone. The cone is connected to the rear of the crankshaft and is used for starting the engine. You will need a starter which has a rubber insert in the business end, and this insert is pushed against the cone before engaging the starter to turn the engine.

You will need to consider whether the design of the helicopter will allow you to use this type of starting method – the undercarriage may make it impossible. You will also need to note that the starter turns in the opposite direction when using this method. Most starters can be reversed simply by connecting the battery leads the other way round, but, if your starter has a one-way bearing fitted, it will not work when reversed and you will need to buy another starter (starters fitted with one-way bearings are available with a choice of starting directions).

Ringed or ABC

The other decision with which you may be confronted is whether to use either what is often referred to as a ringed engine, or an ABC. The piston of the ringed engine is fitted with a conventional piston ring, which seals the gap between the piston and the cylinder wall. The unringed, or ABC, engine uses a combination of special materials and a slightly tapered cylinder to achieve the same result.

The term ABC (which stands for aluminium, brass, chrome) has become generic and is often used to describe any unringed engine with a tapered liner, whatever the materials used in manufacture. However, you should note that an ABC engine is not simply an engine to which no piston ring is fitted but is one which uses the combination of special materials and a tapered bore to achieve a good piston seal throughout its operating temperature range.

If you remove the glow plug from a ringed engine and then turn the crankshaft, you will feel no change in resistance as the piston goes through its full cycle. If you do this with an ABC engine, you will feel a marked resistance as the piston passes top dead centre – this is the point at which the cylinder wall is tapered. If you now refit the plug, you may find that it is very difficult to turn the ABC engine through top dead centre and this can cause a problem when starting a helicopter. If you are buying a helicopter which uses a belt starting system, I suggest that you use a ringed engine, because the difference in performance is minimal and of no significance when you are learning. If you decide to buy an ABC engine, take the engine out of the box and turn it over by hand – if it tends to jam at top dead centre, try another one, because individual engines do vary. If you can't find one which you can turn over by hand, don't buy one. The problem is slightly less with helicopters which use a top start system because you can use a bigger starter or a bigger battery, whereas there is no way of improving the turning power of the starting belt on the flywheel.

The two-stroke glow engine

All the current range of smaller helicopters are designed to use two-stroke engines. It may be possible to fit a four-stroke if you want to, but this usually involves considerable modification to the helicopter as well as a possible change of gear ratios (and most small helicopters do not have alternative gear ratios).

The engine consists of the crankcase, to which is bolted the front housing, and the cylinder head. The front housing has two bearings which support the crankshaft and, for helicopter use, these should both be ballraces. The rear of the crankshaft has a crankpin which takes the big end of the connecting rod, and the little end of the connecting rod is connected to the piston by the gudgeon pin. The cylinder section of the crankcase is fitted with a liner in which the piston slides. The cylinder head is bolted to the top of the crankcase

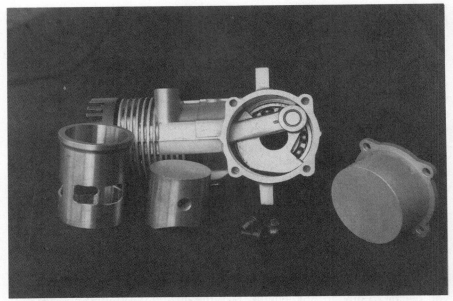

Figure 5.2 *With the backplate removed, the rear ballrace, crankpin and connecting rod are visible, as are the ports in the cylinder liner. This is an ABC engine with no piston ring.*

and it both seals the cylinder and clamps the liner in place. The rear of the crankcase is closed by the backplate, which is fitted with a gasket and held in place with bolts, and the crankcase is then effectively sealed so that it can act as a pump. The glow plug is screwed into the cylinder head and provides the ignition source both for starting and for running. The only other component is the carburettor, which is fitted to the front housing (which can an integral part of the crankcase on some types of engine, instead of being removable).

The major advantages of the two-stroke engine are the small number of moving parts and the lack of anything which needs to be adjusted. The other alternative is the four-stroke and, while it is suitable for use with some helicopters, the cost and complexity make it somewhat of an unnecessary luxury for the novice. The advantages of the four-stroke are the different noise, which may be less offensive, and the improved fuel consumption, which is offset by the much higher initial cost.

Both two-stroke and four-stroke model engines run on a fuel which contains a proportion of lubricating oil. Unlike the car engine, there is no other source of lubrication.

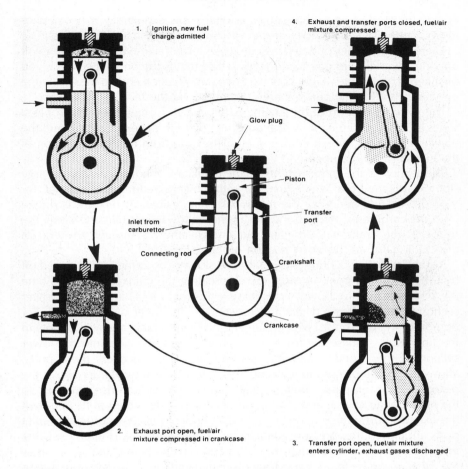

1. Ignition, new fuel charge admitted

4. Exhaust and transfer ports closed, fuel/air mixture compressed

Glow plug

Piston

Transfer port

Inlet from carburettor

Connecting rod

Crankshaft

Crankcase

2. Exhaust port open, fuel/air mixture compressed in crankcase

3. Transfer port open, fuel/air mixture enters cylinder, exhaust gases discharged

Figure 5.3 *Operation of a two-stroke engine. Although the fuel inlet from the carburettor is shown on the side of the engine – for graphical purposes – it would normally enter from the hollow crankshaft.*

How does it work?

The two-stroke engine is so called because it completes its entire cycle in only two movements of the piston, one up and one down. This means that the cylinder fires on every revolution of the crankshaft, unlike the four-stroke which fires on every other revolution. Since a two-stroke typically runs at up to 50 per cent higher rpm than the equivalent four-stroke, the result is an engine which fires up to three times as often. This explains why two-strokes always sound as though they are revving much faster than four-strokes.

There are two types of two-stroke engines – front and rear induction. I will only deal with the front induction type, since that is the only type which you are likely to encounter in helicopters. The rear induction engine uses the same principles but the fuel air mixture is admitted via the rear of the engine.

The cylinder section of the engine is fitted with a steel liner which has a series of ports machined in it. The ports line up with the exhaust stub and the transfer chambers, which convey fuel air mixture from the lower section of the crankcase to the upper.

The section of the crankshaft inside the crankcase is hollow and has a large slot towards the front, which lines up with the carburettor mount so that, for a predetermined period of the rotational cycle, a fuel air mixture is drawn from the carburettor through the slot in the hollow crankshaft and along the inside of the crankshaft. The fuel air charge emerges through the end of the crankshaft into the lower section of the crankcase.

As the crankshaft continues to rotate, the slot moves round and is closed off by the side of the front housing, thereby sealing the crankcase. At this time the piston is moving down, compressing the fuel air mixture in the lower section of the crankcase. There are chambers, in the inner face of the cylinder portion of the crankcase, which connect the lower crankcase with outlets in the liner wall – these are the transfer ports. The ports open into the lower section of the cylinder, and the descending piston uncovers these ports, allowing the compressed fuel air mixture to flow into the cylinder above the piston. The piston passes bottom dead centre and starts to rise, pushing up the new fuel air charge and closing off first the transfer (inlet) ports and then the exhaust port, which is higher up the cylinder wall. As soon as the inlet ports are closed, the pressure starts to fall in the crankcase, thereby sucking more fuel air mixture through the carburettor for the next cycle. As soon as the exhaust port is closed, the cylinder is sealed and the fuel air mixture is then compressed until the combination of heat and pressure, with the catalytic action of the glow plug, results in combustion of the charge as the piston reaches top dead centre. The explosion drives the piston down, uncovering the exhaust port and starting to compress the new fuel air charge in the lower crankcase. The exhaust gases are under pressure and now escape through the exhaust port, aided by the flow of fresh fuel air mixture which enters under crankcase pressure as soon as the transfer ports are uncovered.

You will appreciate that the lack of moving valves means that the system is less efficient at low speeds where the ports are uncovered simultaneously. However, at high rpm the flow of the gases becomes faster and more predictable and the intake and exhaust processes are much more effective. Small two-strokes typically operate most efficiently between twelve and eighteen thousand rpm, whereas comparable four-strokes will operate at around two-thirds of these figures.

The designer of the engine will decide on the relevant opening periods of the ports and the bore/stroke ratio of the engine, and these will determine the engine's performance. The only adjustments which you will be required to make are to the two needles on the carburettor.

The carburettor

The purpose of the carburettor is to deliver a mixture, consisting of 4.5 parts of air to 1 part of methanol, to the engine. The amount of that mixture being delivered is regulated by the throttle, which controls the power output of the engine. The carburettor has two adjustment needles which let you vary the fuel air ratio within fairly narrow limits, outside which the engine simply will not run. If the mixture has more than 4.5 parts of air, it is referred to as being lean and if it has less than 4.5 parts of air, it is referred to as being rich – since the mixture needles adjust the fuel, it is easier to remember this as lean is too little fuel, rich is too much fuel.

If an engine is running rich at full throttle, it will not develop full power and it will cough and splutter and may even stop, but it will suffer no damage because it will not overheat. If an engine is running lean at full throttle, it will develop more power at first but it will rapidly overheat and may seize. Helicopter engines should always be run slightly rich, as you will see.

The moving part of the carburettor consists of a rotating barrel, which not only turns but also moves horizontally, through which air can be drawn when the hole in the barrel lines up with the throat of the carburettor. If you look into the carburettor air intake, you will see the rotating barrel and the open area of the barrel is a measure of the throttle setting. However, when half the area is open the engine will actually be developing about two-thirds of full power. When the throttle is fully closed, you should not be able to see the hole in the barrel at all – in this condition, not only is air unable to enter the carburettor but the sideways movement of the barrel has also closed off the fuel supply at the metering needle (it is necessary for the fuel supply to be shut off for the engine to stop reliably, and this may mean that the barrel has to be turned slightly past the point where the hole ceases to be visible). When the throttle is fully open, the hole in the barrel should be aligned with the throat of the carburettor and, if you look into the throat, you will be able to see the fuel spray bar.

If you turn the throttle arm, you will feel that it meets resistance at each end of its travel. The full throttle point is fixed, but there may be an adjustment screw for the idle point. This will usually consist of a small screw with a lock nut, although it is often omitted on helicopter carburettors. You should check that the barrel closes completely when the throttle is against the stop and you should adjust the stop if necessary to achieve this. If the throttle does not close sufficiently, because the stop is badly adjusted, you will be unable to shut down the engine at the end of a flight and you will have to remove the fuel tube, which can be fiddly.

Setting up a carburettor

The first thing to do is to read the instructions which came with the engine. However, these are often not as helpful as they might be, particularly if you cannot persuade the engine to start in the first place. Manufacturers and distributors claim that they supply the engine with the carburettor already adjusted to a setting where the engine will run. First, they don't always do so, and secondly, you may not be dealing with a new engine.

You will note that I have said that it is necessary to fly the helicopter on full throttle in order to set the main needle accurately, and I realise that you may not have reached that stage yet – do not despair. When the model is in the hover, the settings of both needles will have an effect but, if you follow the method laid out below, the idle needle should be set correctly. This means that, if the engine does not run well in the hover, you need to adjust only the main needle. You will probably find that the setting range will not be particularly critical and, while you may be running the engine under conditions which would not necessarily be quite right for full power, that won't matter if you are only hovering the helicopter.

If you are doubtful about which adjustment screw is which, the instructions which came with the motor should help to sort everything out. On a conventional carburettor which uses two mixture screws, screwing either of them in leans the relevant setting, and out richens it – if you have a carburettor which uses an air screw as opposed to a fuel screw (and I don't know of any that are fitted to helicopter engines, but the instructions should make it clear which it is), what follows does not apply and you should seek help. One other point which you may note about the needles is that the idle adjustment is very sensitive and should be moved only in very small amounts, whereas the main needle can be adjusted over quite a wide range. However, this is not always the case and you should confine yourself to adjustments of no more than a few degrees until you have some experience with the particular carburettor.

In the club of which I am a member, we have recently had two new engines, from different manufacturers, whose carburettors had been so badly set that there was absolutely no chance of the engines starting, let alone running. One carburettor had the idle needle screwed in so that no fuel could flow at all and the other had both the needles set so rich that fuel kept being blown out of the silencer. This meant that it was necessary to reset the idle needles from scratch.

This exercise is simplest if you remove the carburettor from the engine, and all you will need is about three or four inches of clean fuel tubing. First, attach the tubing to the fuel nipple, then screw the main needle in gently until it bottoms and unscrew it about five turns so that it is not going to affect the next bit. Set the throttle so that there is an opening of about ¹⁄₁₆ " when you look into the barrel – you can adjust the throttle stop screw to hold this if that makes it easier. Now blow through the tubing and adjust the idle screw so that air will just flow. Next screw the main needle in gently until it bottoms and unscrew it about 1½ turns. Refit the carburettor.

The engine should now start, so let it warm up with the glow supply still connected. If it stops as soon as you remove the glow supply, screw in the idle needle until the engine just runs without the glow supply.

The next bit involves flying the helicopter at full power to set the main needle, which, using the above settings, should now be slightly on the rich side. Lean it off carefully to obtain more power if necessary, but take care not to set it too lean. If the engine shows any sign of slowing up at full power, throttle back, land and richen the main needle. If this makes the situation worse (normally it doesn't, but sometimes, particularly if you are using a tuned pipe, it can be difficult to differentiate between too lean and too rich), then you should lean the main needle setting until the engine runs reliably.

Final adjustments to the idle needle are done by checking the pickup when the throttle is opened quickly. If the motor splutters then accelerates, lean the idle needle. If the motor splutters then dies, richen the idle needle.

All this sounds easy if you read it quickly but there is no substitute for experience, so do please ask for help if you are at all unsure.

Glow plugs

The glow plug is screwed into the cylinder head and looks like a miniature version of a car spark plug. If you remove the plug and look at the inner end, you will see a coil of wire which disappears into the interior of the plug and this is the element. The plug may have a small metal bar across the inner end – this is called an idle bar and there is a lot of debate about whether it is a useful addition, although I don't find any advantage in using plugs of this type. The element forms part of an electrical circuit between the post of the plug and its body and if you connect your glow battery across the plug, the element should glow red to orange. If the element is very bright or white hot, you should use a longer connecting lead to the battery, in order to reduce the voltage across the plug. Don't leave the battery connected for more than a few seconds while holding the plug, because the body of the plug will become very hot.

The glow plug provides the ignition source for starting the engine and keeping it running. However, it is only necessary to apply a voltage to the plug while starting the engine because the heat of combustion will keep the element hot enough when the engine is running. The element acts as a catalyst, unlike the spark of a petrol engine, and the engine will run reasonably well even when the element is broken. However, the element must be intact for the heating current to pass when you are starting the engine.

Most plugs nowadays are rated at 1.5 volts which is very unhelpful and apparently stems from the ready availability of large dry batteries somewhere (but not in the UK). However, aided by the low internal resistance of nicads, a single nicad cell (which is nominally 1.2 volts) is quite capable of providing the necessary current for starting the engine. The alternative is a single lead-acid cell (which is nominally 2 volts) with a long lead to reduce the voltage. Typical glow plug currents are between 2.5 amps and 5 amps, depending on the plug, the voltage and whether the element is wet with fuel.

Figure 5.4 *A glow plug with the element clearly visible.*

There is no need to change the plug routinely. Most plug failures occur when the glow power is first connected, which is why an ammeter in the circuit is useful, because you will see that no current is passing when you have connected the power source. Within my experience, if the plug fails in the air, all that will happen is that the engine will start to run slightly rough – I have never had this cause an engine to stop.

So which plug should you use? If you have found one which is reliable, stick to it. I don't want to start a debate about the merits of various plugs but if you need to buy a new plug, ask your model shop for an OS 8 or an Enya 3 or, failing either, an equivalent and your engine will run satisfactorily. Oh, and keep a spare plug handy – it's the best insurance I know against having the one in the model fail.

Fuel and what goes in it

The glow fuel which you buy will consist of two or three components. Methanol is the ingredient which actually burns and provides the power source, oil is added as a lubricant and heat dispersant, and there may be additional performance enhancers of which nitromethane ('nitro') is the most common.

When it comes to choosing your fuel, you should be guided by the instructions which are supplied with the engine. All the small two-strokes used in helicopters will run on a mixture of methanol, 20% castor oil, and up to 10% nitro. Some should not be run on more than 2% nitro, others benefit from up to 10%, but the instructions will tell you what to use.

The other decision which you may face is whether to use fuel containing synthetic oil. The advantages of synthetic oil are that it has a much cleaner exhaust residue than castor (partly because it is used in lower proportions) and that the engine will produce slightly more power. The main disadvantage is that it breaks down at a lower temperature and so gives less protection against the overheating resulting from a lean engine run.

The safest course for the beginner is to use a fuel containing 75% methanol, 20% castor and 5% nitro (unless the instructions tell you to use less). This mixture will give you good protection against lean running, and the nitro will give easier starting and better slow running. When you have gained some experience with small glow engines, you can experiment with alternative mixtures, although the cost of nitro will be a deterrent against going much above 10%. The disadvantage of nitro (apart from the cost) is that its combustion produces nitric acid, which corrodes the bearings in a model engine. However, the induction system of a two-stroke ensures that the crankcase is regularly flushed with fresh fuel, so this is not much of a problem. It is a different matter with four-strokes, however, because the fuel comes in via the inlet valve and does not pass through the crankcase at all.

Silencers, mufflers and tuned pipes

The British use silencers on their engines and mufflers round their necks, the Americans use mufflers for both. Unfortunately, the one thing which you cannot avoid noticing is that silencers don't, so perhaps mufflers is the more accurate description and that is what I will call them. After at least five years of noise testing all types of small helicopters, I have found that the average noise reading is around 78dbA, when using the BMFA test criteria with the helicopter in the hover and the meter seven metres away. The exception is the Kyosho Concept which, when fitted with an aero muffler as the instructions suggest, invariably exceeds the 82dbA limit. The small area over which helicopters fly when you are learning means that noise is not usually a problem, but this can change if you start flying a sixty-powered machine or doing aerobatics and you should not ignore it. If you join a club, the committee will probably test helicopters and insist that they are silenced to comply with the BMFA limit.

You will notice that helicopter engines do not come with mufflers and this is because of the variations which arise in the different installations. However, many helicopter kits do include a muffler and the degree of standardisation amongst the 30 range of engines virtually guarantees that it will fit whatever motor you may decide to use.

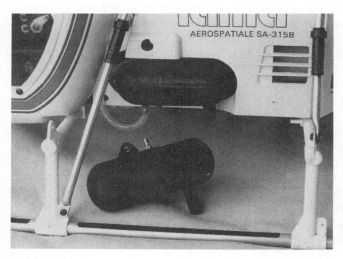

Figure 5.5 *Two standard helicopter mufflers, the lower one fits the My Star 30.*

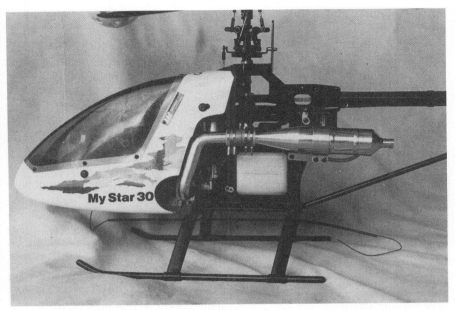

Figure 5.6 *My Star 30 fitted with a Hatori tuned pipe.*

Using a tuned pipe

I recommend that you stick to using the standard muffler until you are accustomed to the handling of the engine, because tuned pipes do have characteristics
of their own, but, if you find that you need to quieten the helicopter still
further, a tuned pipe can do this. The main purpose of a tuned pipe is to
increase the power output from the engine and this is normally achieved by
increasing the rpm as well as fitting the pipe. However, a pipe can improve
the silencing and also give a small increase in power as well, providing you
do not increase the engine rpm significantly.

If you decide to use a tuned pipe, the first point to bear in mind is the rpm
range at which the pipe is designed to work. While helicopter pipes are
generally fairly soft, that is they do not have a very narrow rev band over
which they work, they do require the engine to be run at 16,000 rpm or
more for the best effect. This will probably mean running the rotor head at
a minimum of 1600 rpm. Hatori quote 18,000 rpm for their pipes and this is
a typical figure for most manufacturers. I usually run a new engine on a
standard muffler for a few tanks of fuel, in order to set it up and run it in. This

also allows me to assess how much performance improvement is achieved by the use of the pipe.

The first problem can arise when fuelling the model. If you use a tuned pipe, you will probably also be using exhaust pressurisation of the fuel tank. The design of many of the pipes around means that if you overfill the tank and the surplus fuel then goes back up the pressure line to the tuned pipe, the fuel promptly runs back down the manifold and in through the exhaust port of the engine. You will now find that the engine will not turn over when the starter is applied, because you are trying to compress a liquid. Persistence may well bend the connecting rod. The cure is to turn the model so that the engine exhaust port is facing downwards, then to turn the flywheel backwards and forwards by hand to allow the fuel to escape from the cylinder. You will now need to rotate the whole helicopter in order to drain the fuel back up the manifold and out through the tuned pipe. It may be simpler to remove the glow plug and use the starter to blow the fuel out of the plug hole. The best solution is to remove the fuel tube from the pressure nipple when refuelling, so that the surplus fuel does not go into the pipe in the first place.

Having fuelled the model, I set the main needle about half a turn richer than for the standard muffler and then start it in the usual way. The engine should idle with no change to the low needle setting and you can now try the hover. Depending on how fast you are running the head, you may find little change in the hover, but if you find the head speed has reduced you should lean out the main needle to bring it back. You can now try full power, opening the throttle fairly slowly and being prepared to close it slightly and land the model if the engine starts to object. Hopefully you will find that you can fly round on full power with no problem, so you should keep the throttle wide open for up to a minute, then close it for a rapid descent. If the engine does not throttle back immediately but stays on a high power setting, or even starts to scream its head off because it is now running on little load, the engine is overheating and you need to richen the main needle. You may find that there is quite a wide range of main needle settings over which the engine will perform well and that the adjustment is less critical than when using a standard muffler. Always err on the side of running rich, it makes for longer engine life and less involuntary autorotation practice.

You now need to fly the model around and reset the throttle and pitch curves to use the extra power, while keeping the head speed constant at whatever value you prefer. The idle needle may need to be adjusted slightly, to give a smooth tick-over with just a hint of a rich hesitation occasionally. If the engine just dies when you open the throttle, the idle setting is too rich, if it accelerates then dies, it is too lean.

The experts generally use lower head speeds for hovering manoeuvres, which makes the model easier to fly accurately, and higher head speeds for aerobatics, which makes the model more responsive. This also means that the tuned pipe is working more efficiently when the extra power is required for the aerobatics. You do, of course, need a transmitter with separate throttle/pitch curves to do this, not simply an idle up setting.

Care and maintenance

There isn't much that needs to be done to look after a two-stroke if you are using it regularly. There are various products on the market which can be used for preventing corrosion if the engine is not being run , but it is very difficult to use them when the engine is installed in the helicopter and it isn't necessary unless you are planning to lay the engine up for some months. If you are using a fuel with castor oil, you may notice that the engine is difficult to turn over when it has stood for a while. This is because castor oil dries out to leave a sticky residue, but this will soon dissolve in fresh fuel and causes no harm. If the engine is difficult to turn over at first, after a period of non-use, don't fly the model immediately or attempt to adjust the mixture – let the engine run at a high rpm on the ground for a minute or two to wash away the residue.

If you are going to lay the helicopter up for the winter, the best plan would be to remove the engine from the model, and this isn't difficult because you can take it out complete with the clutch shoes and fan. You can then use one of the commercial after-run products as directed and this will prevent corrosion of the bearings.

If you are using the engine regularly, eventually (years, not months) it will need maintenance. The symptoms will be a loss of power or difficult starting and this will probably be due either to wear or to carbon build up. You can return the engine to the distributors or their servicing agents, or you can buy a book which will go into detail on the care and maintenance of model engines.

CHAPTER 6

Everything you need to know about radio systems

What you need, how it works, why helicopter radios are different and what they do, and gyros

Buying your first radio control system is just as difficult as buying your first model. It is also a decision which is likely to have a more lasting influence on your modelling career because you will probably continue to use the same radio system for many years and many models.

Modern radio control systems are all reliable and there is little to choose between them from that point of view. As far as the quality and level of sophistication are concerned, you will get what you pay for and the more you spend, the more facilities the radio will include.

Figure 6.1 *Three helicopter computer transmitters. On the left is the JR PCM-10, which uses a touch screen for programming. The Futaba Field Force Super 7 and the JR X-388S are multi-function transmitters.*

The radio system

The radio system consists of the transmitter, the receiver, the servos, and the various additional bits and pieces which are necessary to make it work, such as the batteries, crystals, charger and switch harness. If you buy a 'combo', it will contain everything apart from the servos. You may also be offered the choice of 'nicads' or 'dry batteries'. A system which uses nicads (short for nickel cadmium cells), which are rechargeable, will include the necessary charger. A dry battery system will be cheaper but will only include plastic holders into which you will need to fit standard dry batteries – you will need eight for the transmitter and four for the receiver and I will go into more detail later.

The pilot holds the transmitter, and the receiver and servos are installed in the model, the servos being plugged into their appropriate receiver sockets and connected mechanically to their appropriate model flying controls. The transmitter takes the positions of the various control sticks, knobs and switches and converts them into a series of radio signals which are then sent to the receiver. The receiver decodes the signals and sends each one to its appropriate servo, which then moves to the position demanded by the setting of the transmitter control. All the various transmitter controls are checked about twenty-five times every second and the servos are moved as necessary.

Radio systems are usually available either for fixed-wing models or for helicopters. The only significant difference between the two is the transmitter – in fact, that is usually the only difference. The current range of multi-function systems, such as the MacGregor/JR X-3810 and X-388S, and the Futaba Field Force 7, can be set by the pilot for either use and they are only available in one (universal) configuration.

You can assume that all the radio equipment from any one manufacturer will be compatible. You will be able to buy another receiver or more servos, or another transmitter, and it will all work together (the exception being that a PPM transmitter will not operate a PCM receiver, of which more later). However, it is much wiser to assume that one manufacturer's products (transmitters and receivers in particular) will not work with those from another manufacturer. Gyros are an exception and are often interchangeable (providing you can control the gain) and there are manufacturers who produce equipment, including servos and receivers, which can be used universally (although you may need to specify which connecting lead you require). The safest assumption is that you can't mix makes unless the manufacturer (**not** the club expert) specifically says you can. If you are using a transmitter and receiver from different manufacturers, check which crystals should be used in each piece of equipment.

AM and FM, PCM and PPM, and dual conversion

I think it is a good idea to dispose of the jargon straight away. You will come across these terms and, while you should know their significance, there is no need for a technical understanding of what they mean.

AM and FM

AM stands for **amplitude modulation**, FM stands for **frequency modulation**, and they are terms which describe the way in which the control information is carried by the radio signal. All current 35MHz radio systems use FM and it is a built-in part of the system over which you have no control.

PCM and PPM

PCM stands for **pulse code modulation** and PPM stands for **pulse proportional modulation**. PPM is what radios used to use and it had no name until PCM came along, when it became necessary to tell the two apart. PCM and PPM describe the two alternative ways in which the control stick positions are measured and the information is processed – PPM is an analogue system which uses varying voltages and PCM is a digital one which uses numbers. Theoretically, what is called a 1024 system can achieve a resolution which corresponds to about one-eighth of a degree of servo movement but, unfortunately, only the most expensive servos can actually achieve this accuracy.

Receivers are either PCM or PPM, whereas PCM transmitters can be switched to PPM if you want to use a PPM receiver. There are several technical arguments as to why PCM provides a more reliable radio link with the model but the main one which will concern you is the fact that you must use a PCM receiver if you want to use failsafe (which is dealt with in Chapter 11). PPM radio systems do not have integral failsafe.

MacGregor/JR radio systems use two types of PCM, called SPCM and ZPCM – SPCM is the later version and is a 1024 system, whereas ZPCM is 512. However, SPCM transmitters can be switched to ZPCM as well as PPM.

Dual conversion

The main advantage of dual conversion receivers (there is no such thing as a dual conversion transmitter) is that they are claimed to eliminate a theoretical cause of interference between the low channel numbers (see below) and those twenty-three above them – 60 interferes with 83, 61 with 84, and 62 with

85 (but not the other way round). To date, I understand that this interference has never been demonstrated on the flying field and the theory apparently indicates that it would be very unlikely to occur anyway. Even if the theory is correct, it would seem that there would be no point in using a dual conversion receiver unless you wanted to fly on 83, 84 or 85 and someone else was flying on the channel twenty-three below you.

Dual conversion receivers were originally developed for use in America on the 72MHz band, where the problem is, apparently, more acute.

Frequency allocation

Within the UK there are three VHF frequency bands in use for radio control, that is to say there are three groups of frequencies which are used, each group being contained within a span of less than 1MHz (megahertz). The bands are 27MHz, 35MHz and 40MHz. 40MHz is only available for 'ground vehicles', i.e. boats, cars, hovercraft, motorbikes and anything else you can think of which doesn't fly. 27MHz is available for anything, but unfortunately that includes some CB channels, so for practical purposes, 27MHz is no use as far as we are concerned. 35MHz is restricted to flying models only and that is the band in use almost universally – there is a UHF band as well but you are unlikely to find many modellers who use it.

Within the 35MHz band, which extends from 35.000MHz to 35.250MHz, there are 26 individual frequencies, or channels as they are usually called, each of which can be used for flying one model at a time. The channels are numbered from 60 to 85 and it is by these channel numbers that the frequencies are identified. However, you may find that the transmitter crystal only has the frequency on its label and you will have to convert this to the channel. The 26 frequencies are from 35.000MHz to 35.250MHz in 10kHz (kilohertz) steps, i.e. 35.000, 35.010, 35.020, 35.030 and so on, channel 60 being 35.000MHz. To work out what the channel number is, take 35 away from the frequency, ignore the last zero, and add 60 to what is left – if the frequency is 35.090MHz, add 9 to 60 and that is channel 69, and if the frequency is 35.200MHz, add 20 to 60 and that is channel 80. If you can't remember this, you should make a note of it because it is absolutely vital that you should be certain which channel you are using. Many accidents are caused every year by confusion over frequencies and it is amazing how many people do not understand what they are doing – I have asked many fliers over the years which channel they are using, only to be told either that they don't know or that they are using 35MHz.

Crystals are supplied in pairs, marked with the channel and either Tx or Rx.

The crystal marked Tx goes in the transmitter and the crystal marked Rx goes in the receiver – the radio will not work if you swap them over.

Frequencies and channel numbers

At risk of labouring the point, I have included a table to convert frequencies into channels.

Frequency (MHz)	Channel
35.000	60
35.010	61
35.020	62
35,030	63
35.040	64
35.050	65
35.060	66
35.070	67
35.080	68
35.090	69
35.100	70
35.110	71
35.120	72
35.130	73
35.140	74
35.150	75
35.160	76
35.170	77
35.180	78
35.190	79
35.200	80
35.210	81
35.220	82
35.230	83
35.240	84
35.250	85

A small technical point

For those of you who may be interested, the frequency quoted on the crystal is the frequency on which the transmitter will operate when that crystal is inserted – it is not the frequency of the crystal itself but is a multiple of it.

The same is true of the receiver crystal, and a crystal for a dual-conversion receiver will not be the same frequency as one for a standard receiver. I only include this information in case you have access to a crystal frequency checker and are puzzled as to why it apparently gives the wrong figure. When the transmitter is switched on, a spectrum analyser or transmitter frequency checker will show the frequency which is stated on the crystal.

The only point you need to remember is that the transmitter and the receiver must be fitted with crystals with the same channel number or frequency marked on them for the radio to work, and those crystals must be in their appropriate places, Tx in the transmitter and Rx in the receiver.

Using the various frequencies

The reason that I have written at some length about frequencies is that you cannot operate two transmitters on the same frequency at the same time. It does not matter whether they are FM, AM, PCM or PPM, or any combination of these – if they are on the same frequency, they will interfere with one another and the models will both crash. There are no exceptions to this rule.

All model clubs will have some form of frequency allocation and control and they will insist that you comply with this, for your own safety and that of other fliers.

Figure 6.2 The back of a modular transmitter with the module removed. The Tx crystal is channel 62 and the frequency flag is clearly visible attached to the transmitter.

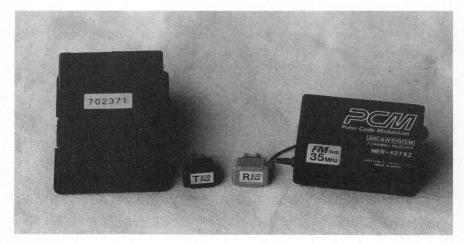

Figure 6.3 *Transmitter module and receiver with their respective crystals.*

Modular transmitters

You may buy what is called a modular transmitter. This is fitted with a removable plug-in section, the module, which contains the electronics for the radio frequency transmission. The module determines the frequency band, so that you can buy a 27MHz module or a 35MHz module or a 40MHz module. The crystal is then plugged into the module and the crystal determines the channel within that band. Each band has its own crystals and you cannot use the crystals from one band in the module for another band.

Most of the more expensive transmitters use removable modules and this can be convenient if you are going to another country and want to use the local frequency band, because you only need to buy the appropriate module and crystals. However, there are no modular receivers (because the cost of the receiver module alone would be too high when compared with the cost of a complete non-modular receiver), so you will have to buy another receiver as well.

Computer radios, and their memories

Computer radios are not computers and you do not need to know anything whatsoever about programming in order to use one. The term is often applied to the complete radio system but it is only the transmitter which is different.

All older transmitters, and some of the current more basic ones, have small rotary potentiometers (pots) which are used for setting up the auxiliary control functions. These are usually hidden behind a panel and they are operated using a special tool or a small screwdriver, and there will also be several small sliding switches. When you are adjusting these pots, the only indication you have of the setting is the angle which the screwdriver slot makes with a small scale around it. If you want to use the transmitter to fly two models, it is impossible to reset these pots accurately when changing models and it is very easy to forget either one of the pots or one of the sliding switches.

Computer transmitters have the normal flying controls but all the pots and sliding switches are replaced by a screen on which the actual settings for each of the controls may be displayed, usually as a percentage. The various functions are selected and changes are made to the settings by use of a series of keys, or by a touch screen. The more advanced transmitters have graphical displays which enable you to watch the change in the servo position as the transmitter controls are operated.

A further bonus with the computer transmitter may be the availability of two or more model memories. When you put all the details of one particular model into the transmitter, all the information is stored in one memory. This will include the stick mode, receiver type, control movements and directions, and anything else which the transmitter allows you to adjust. The memory has a number and can usually also be named to make it easier to remember. When you want to fly that model, all you need to do is to select that model's memory, by pressing the keys on the front of the transmitter until its name is shown on the screen. A second model's details can be stored in a second memory and so on, with the information in each memory being completely independent.

You have probably spotted the fact that, whereas you could forget to change over the odd switch or two when changing models with a non-computer transmitter, armed with a computer version you can forget to change memories and then take-off with **all** the controls reversed (except, presumably, the throttle). Unfortunately, like computers everywhere, computer transmitters will only do what you tell them, not what you meant to tell them, so the usual before take-off waggle of the controls is still a good idea.

The main transmitter controls

Radio control transmitters which are designed for flying models all have a minimum of two control sticks which operate four control functions. Each control stick moves in two axes simultaneously and each axis controls one of the two control functions.

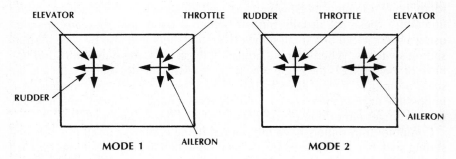

ELEVATOR   THROTTLE   RUDDER   THROTTLE   ELEVATOR

RUDDER

AILERON

MODE 1   AILERON   MODE 2

Figure 6.4 *These are the most popular transmitter modes.*

The four basic control functions are **throttle, rudder, elevator** and **aileron**. Which control function is controlled by which stick movement is determined by the Mode of the transmitter. Probably the most common Mode in use in the UK is Mode 2, in which fore and aft movement of the left stick controls the throttle position and left and right movement of the left stick controls the rudder position. Fore and aft movement of the right stick controls the elevator position and left and right movement of the right stick controls the aileron position.

When the left stick is moved in the fore and aft direction, it is commonly referred to as the throttle stick whereas when it is moved in the left and right direction, it is referred to as the rudder stick. The same applies to the right stick, which may be called either the aileron stick or the elevator stick, but in either case there is only one stick and you should not be confused by this terminology. The aileron, elevator and rudder sticks will be fitted with self-centring springs, whereas the throttle stick will be fitted with some sort of friction or ratchet device.

The other Mode which you may see in use is Mode 1, where the elevator and throttle functions are transposed. There are two further Modes, 3 and 4, which are left-handed versions of Modes 2 and 1 respectively, but these are very uncommon.

Some radios can have the Mode altered by the user whereas some have to be ordered in the required configuration. However, those radios which can have the Mode changed are not designed for this to be a simple process which can be carried out at the flying field – it is intended that you should set the Mode when you buy the radio, although you can change it later if necessary. When deciding which Mode to choose, you should bear in mind that anyone who teaches you or helps to set up your helicopter may need to fly your model using your radio and he will be unable to do so unless you are using the Mode to which he is accustomed.

The direction of operation of the controls seems self evident but has been known to lead to confusion, so here is a quick explanation of what will happen, starting with the helicopter in a level hover. When you move the rudder stick to the left, the model will turn to the left, that is to say, the nose of the model will go to the left but the tail of the model (very obviously with a helicopter) will go to the right. Pushing the elevator stick forwards will make the nose of the model go down, whereas pulling it back will make the nose of the model come up. Moving the aileron stick to the left will make the model lean, or roll, to the left and vice versa. Finally, pushing the throttle stick forwards will increase the power setting and increase the collective pitch, making the heli-copter climb vertically, whereas pulling the throttle stick back will reduce the throttle setting and reduce the collective pitch, making the helicopter descend vertically.

Incidentally, if you fly full-size helicopters you may feel that it is natural to pull back on the throttle stick in order to apply power and climb the model – I did. However, please don't set the model up so that this is what happens, because you will have all sorts of problems with the transmitter mixing. The only exception to this is if you are using one of the very advanced computer transmitters which have throttle **stick** reversing as an option (that is not the same as throttle **servo** reversing).

Secondary transmitter controls

The transmitter will also have additional controls. Beside each of the control sticks there will be sliding levers, which are the trimmers. These provide a small amount of adjustment to the appropriate servo position and are used for day to day trimming of the model's flying controls so that it flies 'hands-off'. The throttle trimmer is used to adjust the engine idling speed and also to reduce the throttle setting at the end of the flight until the engine stops. On some transmitters, you may find that the throttle trimmer has no effect when the throttle stick is above the half open position – this is deliberate and it means that you can alter the idling speed of the engine without affecting the full power setting.

The transmitter may also have a number of switches, which may be either two or three position, and a number of rotary controls (sometimes referred to as potentiometers or pots).

There will also be a power ON/OFF switch, which should be protected so that it is not easily knocked either on or off, and a screen which will show information ranging from just the transmitter battery voltage to details of the model, timers and so on.

What is the minimum you need to fly a helicopter?

There are five control functions required for flying a helicopter. These are **throttle, collective pitch, tail rotor pitch, cyclic roll** and **cyclic pitch** but in order to simplify matters I will refer to them by their fixed-wing equivalents from now on, where possible, so they will be called respectively **throttle, collective, rudder, aileron** and **elevator**.

It is clearly necessary to control all five of these functions using only the two sticks (which have only four axes), so it is necessary to combine the throttle and collective functions in some way.

If you are currently flying fixed-wing models using a four-channel radio, it is possible to fly some helicopters using this set-up.

Some models are designed so that you can connect both the throttle linkage and the collective linkage to the same servo output disk, thereby using only four servos. With the exception of the very small number of specialist machines which require CCPM transmitter mixing, all helicopters can be fitted with five servos and flown with the throttle and collective servos connected to the same receiver output by means of a Y-lead. The difficulty with both these methods is that it is only possible to adjust the relationship between the channels by offsetting the mechanical positions and this is never wholly satisfactory. You may also find that the mechanical layout necessitates a reversed servo action, which is impossible to achieve if you are using a Y-lead unless you can have the servo reversed by the manufacturer or your model shop.

While it is possible to fly many helicopters using a basic four-channel fixed-wing set, this is definitely not the best option and you will soon realise the limitations. I would strongly recommend anyone who is including a new radio in their budget for starting helicopter flying to buy a helicopter system. If you are already flying fixed-wing models, you may be able to buy only the transmitter but you will also need five servos and a gyro (about which more later). If you do eventually decide not to continue with helicopters, your transmitter may still be used for fixed-wing models – in fact it is ideal for flying twins where one throttle servo is connected as usual and the other is connected to the collective channel. This enables you to start and set up the engines independently and even to throttle one back in the air to practise single-engined flying.

Figure 6.5 You may find that a transmitter tray is useful but check that you can operate all the controls when using it.

The helicopter transmitter

The ideal relationship between the throttle position and the collective pitch setting will ensure that the main rotor rpm remains constant throughout the range from lift-off to full power. This ensures that the control response remains the same because the control response is directly related to the main rotor rpm. Unfortunately, it is not possible to achieve the ideal relationship simply by opening the throttle at the same time as moving the collective linkage, mainly because the power output from the engine does not change linearly with the movement of the arm attached to the carburettor barrel – typically, a half-open throttle will give about two-thirds of full power.

The throttle and the collective channels are automatically mixed within the helicopter transmitter and both channels are operated by the throttle stick. What a helicopter transmitter also enables you to do is to vary the relationship between the throttle and the collective channels, so as to maintain the ideal match as closely as possible throughout the range of throttle stick positions.

Throttle/collective mixing

The helicopter is always set up mechanically so that it hovers with the throttle stick in the mid position and the main rotor rpm at the correct value, this being achieved by adjusting the linkages in the helicopter. The throttle and collective servos are plugged into the appropriate outlets of the receiver (usually the throttle and one of the auxiliary channels) and both servos will then operate when the throttle stick is moved. If you set the various transmitter adjustments to zero, the two servos will move through the same arc and their relative positions will be the same throughout that arc.

In the simplest system, the movement of the throttle servo is left unchanged but the relative position of the collective servo is altered so that the main rotor blade setting is always what is needed for the power which the engine is producing, whatever the throttle setting. However, this is actually achieved simply by limiting the amount of collective servo movement independently above and below the neutral (hover) point. This will ensure that the main rotor speed is satisfactory at full power, in the hover, and with the throttle closed, but it may well not be as required at any intermediate stick positions.

The more sophisticated transmitters allow you to set the collective pitch at five or more points in the range and this means that the pitch can be much more accurately matched to the power output. You will also have a similar means of altering the position of the throttle servo relative to the stick position, which makes for even more accurate adjustment.

Idle up and throttle hold

A basic helicopter transmitter will probably have a switch labelled *idle up* or something similar. What this does is to enable you to set a minimum setting below which the throttle will not close even though the throttle stick continues to be pulled back. This will prevent the main rotor rpm from decreasing when the throttle stick is pulled back during aerobatics.

The other switch which you may see will be labelled *hold*, or *throttle hold*, and this is used for practising autorotations. Contrary to popular theory, when the engine in a helicopter stops, the machine does not plummet earthwards instantly. What actually happens is that the direction of the airflow through the main rotor is reversed as the machine falls and the upward flow now drives the main rotor like a windmill, because the pilot has reduced the collective setting to a minimum. Since the blades are still developing some lift, the helicopter reaches a stable state with a constant rate of descent but a rapidly rotating main rotor. As the ground approaches, the pilot increases the collective pitch setting so that the main blades produce more lift and the rate of descent is slowed – this of course will result in the kinetic energy of the main rotor reducing, with the blades slowing down because the windmill effect is reduced. The trick lies in running out of kinetic energy at the same time as (or slightly after) the helicopter runs out of height. Incidentally, this is a grossly oversimplified description, not a set of instructions for doing an autorotation so please don't try it.

What throttle hold does is to disconnect the throttle channel from the collective and to leave the throttle stick controlling only the collective. The throttle servo moves to a pre-set position which leaves the engine running at a reliable idle. This means that the pilot can position the model somewhere overhead, then select throttle hold and practise an autorotation – if he decides that it is not working out, all he has to do is to switch throttle hold off and the engine will respond normally, enabling him to climb away and try again.

Revolution mixing, or ATS

The engine of the helicopter drives two rotors. The main rotor provides the lift which supports the machine and it does this by turning the main blades, each of which behaves like a small wing (or, I suppose, a large propeller, depending on your point of view). The result of the rotor turning in one direction is that the fuselage tries to turn in the opposite direction, and this tendency is resisted by the tail rotor. If you are a fan of full-size machines, you will have noted that the other two solutions to this problem are to have two main rotors, like the Chinook, or contra-rotating main rotors like the Kaman range.

The pitch of the tail rotor blades is varied by the rudder stick in order to prevent the fuselage from turning and to control the heading of the helicopter. However, every time that the power setting, and thereby the torque, is changed, the tail rotor setting needs to be changed in order to keep the helicopter's heading constant.

The neutral point from which the revolution mixing is set up is, like the collective pitch, the hover. When the helicopter is in a stable hover, the control linkages are adjusted so that the rudder servo is at neutral and there is sufficient tail rotor pitch applied for the fuselage to maintain a steady heading. The revolution mixing increases the tail rotor pitch as the collective pitch is increased in order to make the helicopter climb, and decreases the tail rotor pitch as the collective pitch is decreased in order to make the helicopter descend. You may note that it is actually the collective pitch setting which is used to change the tail rotor, not the throttle setting, although both are of course controlled by the same stick.

The conventional helicopter transmitter will have either one or two rotary controls which enable you to set the maximum and minimum tail rotor pitch settings which will be achieved as the throttle stick is moved through its full range. The computer transmitter will have the information stored in the model's memory.

CCPM computer mixing

You may come across a reference to this type of mixing, either in the specification for the radio or the helicopter. It stands for **cyclic collective pitch mixing**, or something similar, and it is most commonly used to describe a helicopter in which the servos are connected directly to the swashplate without any intermediate mechanical mixing, the necessary mixing being done in the transmitter. A typical installation, when viewed from above, will have three servos spaced at 120-degree intervals round the swashplate, one being at the front (12 o'clock) and the others being to the left (8 o'clock) and right (4 o'clock). Movement of the collective stick will result in all three servos moving by the same amount. Down elevator will result in the front servo moving the front of the swashplate downwards and the side servos both moving the rear of the swashplate upwards, left roll will result in the front servo not moving at all but the left servo moving the swashplate downwards and the right servo moving it upwards. The advantages of CCPM are the direct linkage and positive control. The disadvantages are that you must have a suitable transmitter and a suitable helicopter, which has been designed to use CCPM.

Gyros

The arrival of the gyro greatly simplified the process of learning to fly a helicopter. What the gyro does is to prevent the tail from swinging, thereby keeping the helicopter on a constant heading and reducing the amount of work which has to be done by the pilot.

The gyro is connected between the rudder servo and the receiver and it draws its power from the receiver in the same way that the servos do. Many gyros have no separate switch and they are turned on and off with the receiver. In its simplest form, a gyro will be a single box with a small adjustment screw, which is used for altering the gain. Reversing of the gyro sense will be done simply by turning it upside down before mounting it in the model.

The current range of mechanical gyros uses a pair of flywheels, which are mounted on a single axle and are driven by an electric motor which is mounted between them. The whole assembly is then mounted on a second axle which is in the same plane as, but at ninety degrees to, the axis of rotation of the flywheels. This axle can rotate in bearings at either end but its movement is restrained by a spring. The result of this arrangement is that turning the whole device in the horizontal plane causes the flywheel assembly to turn about the second axle because of gyroscopic precession. The amount of movement is restricted by the spring and is therefore proportional to the rate of rotation of the model in the yaw axis.

If you take a modern gyro to pieces, you will probably find no obvious means of detecting the displacement, whereas older gyros had potentiometers attached to the moving section. Modern gyros use Hall Effect to detect the motion. A small bar magnet is attached to the moving part and a type of semi-conductor is mounted among the electronics nearby – the peculiar characteristic of this semi-conductor is that its electrical performance is sensitive to any change in the magnetic field surrounding it, and it therefore responds to movements of the bar magnet. This response is the 'error signal' and it is then amplified and used to control the rudder servo. The degree of amplification corresponds to the gain of the gyro.

The gain of the gyro is the amount of authority it exercises over the tail – if the gain is set high, the tail will be more securely held on the heading. However, the gyro's only aim in life is to sense any turn and to oppose it – the gyro doesn't know why the model is turning and doesn't care. The result of this is that a high gain setting makes the tail control less effective because as fast as you apply rudder in one direction to start the model turning, the gyro applies rudder in the opposite direction to stop it. The gain setting therefore becomes a compromise between stability and manoeuvrability.

The gyro does not have any directional sensing. It is of a type called a rate gyro and its response is a product of the rate of rotation of the helicopter and the gain setting – the faster the helicopter turns, the more the gyro will oppose the turn. However, once the helicopter stops turning, the opposing signal from the gyro drops to zero – it is this which enables the pilot to turn the helicopter when he wants to.

The latest gyros are called **solid state** and they use an arrangement of crystals, instead of the spinning weights, to detect the rotation of the helicopter. The elimination of all the moving parts makes the gyro much less prone to damage but, unfortunately, the sophisticated electronics, which are necessary to make this type of detector operate satisfactorily, greatly increase the price.

Which one should you buy?

The simple answer is always "The best you can afford" but knowing how much use you will make of the facilities and whether you will need four or eight or more model memories, when you are first starting, is impossible. However, you may care to take the following points into consideration.

- Do buy a helicopter system if you want to fly helicopters – you can always use it to fly fixed-wing models if you want to.
- Five channels is the minimum, preferably with five servos. A sixth channel is necessary for remote switching of the gyro gain.
- Look for a helicopter radio package – you may be able to find a complete system with five servos and a gyro at an all-in price.
- Don't bother with a dry battery system – you will have spent as much on batteries in the first flying season as it would have cost to have paid the extra for the nicads. The main problem is that you must change the receiver batteries regularly, probably before they are even half used, because you simply cannot take a chance and there is no way of knowing how much charge is remaining.
- Don't be put off by 'computer' sets. They do not require any programming skills and the latest displays mean that you don't need to take the instruction book to the flying field. They are simple to use, it is very easy to set the helicopter up with one, and you don't have to use all the facilities at first.
- The multi-function sets are versatile and can be used for both types of model – they also have some very advanced specialist glider facilities, if you are interested in that aspect of model flying.
- A modular transmitter may be worth considering if you want to fly abroad or if you also want to operate cars or boats on the 40MHz or 27 MHz bands. However, you cannot buy modular receivers.
- Be very careful if you are offered a second-hand system, particularly if the seller seems not to know too much about it. Model radio equipment is stolen every year and someone must be using it. If you buy a package from a shop and get a discount, you will get a new radio for little more than the cost of a good second-hand one.

CHAPTER 7

All about rotor blades

Assembling, finishing and balancing the rotor blades (and making your own balancer)

Nowadays, many kits are supplied with the main blades already assembled and covered, and (sometimes) also balanced. However, when you buy the inevitable replacements, you may well be surprised to discover that it is all left to you and there is no clue as to what to do. This chapter will explain how to assemble wooden blades, and then how to cover and balance all kinds of blades.

When it comes to the balancing, there is the hit-and-miss method of sticking a bit of tape on one blade and seeing if it makes the vibration better or worse, then swapping it over if it makes it worse – the trouble here is that, if you add too much weight, you may have made the light blade into the heavy one and you will never reach a balance. The best solution is to balance the blades before you even fit them to the head (and to do it in the comfort of your own home, on your own balancer).

The various types of main blades

Main blades are available in one of two materials, wood or composite. Composite includes glass or carbon fibre, and polyester or epoxy resin – these blades are normally balanced (or very well matched, which comes to nearly the same thing) by the manufacturer but it is still worth checking.

Assembling wooden blades

You have opened the bag and are confronted with two wooden blades, two lead weights and (possibly) some covering material. Nowadays, most wooden blades are fitted with lead weights in order to improve the handling of the helicopter but not all wooden blades are weighted, so don't worry if you have

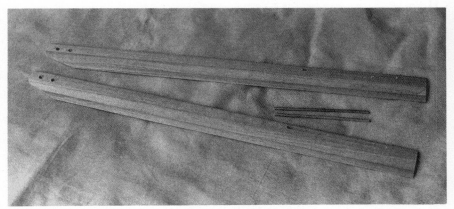

Figure 7.1 *A pair of wooden blades with the slots already routed out, and the lead weights.*

a pair which aren't, just skip the next section and go straight to the one about blade roots.

Fixing the weights

The first task is to stick the weights in the slots which the manufacturer has thoughtfully routed out for you in the hardwood leading edge of each blade. Most manufacturers recommend the use of epoxy adhesive because you need something which will not only stick the weight in the slot but will also fill in the gap around it. If you use epoxy, the five-minute variety is adequate – the weight is restrained by the slot and the epoxy should not be taking the centrifugal loads. I have broken many wooden blades over the years and have never had a weight come loose, even when the blade has broken across the section holding the weight. Pacer Products make a cyano called *Blade Zap*, which is designed specifically for securing blade weights, and this is a good alternative.

Before you actually stick the weight in place, you should take both the strips of lead and check that they will fit into the slots without being forced. If they are too large, file equal amounts off each of them. Next, roll each strip on a flat surface to make it as straight as possible – the aim is to be able to drop the weight into a bed of adhesive and have it settle to the bottom of the slot without being pressed down. If the weight is bent when you drop it in place, you will spend the next five minutes pushing down each end alternately while watching the opposite end emerging again.

The only other item you will need is a roll of Sellotape. Mix up sufficient epoxy to do one blade and pour enough into the slot to cover the bottom. Drop in the weight and, if necessary, press it down with the edge of a ruler (or anything else which will not bend it) so that it is below the surface of the blade. Next, add more adhesive to fill the slot and cover with a strip of Sellotape – this will produce a smooth finish and will shape the adhesive to the profile of the blade. Now do the second blade and leave them both until the adhesive is completely cured. If you are using *Blade Zap*, the procedure is similar. Incidentally, I have found that cyano reacts with the adhesive on masking tape to leave a sticky mess – this does not happen with Sellotape. When the adhesive has cured, remove the tape and, if necessary, sand the area lightly to produce a smooth curve.

Blade roots

If the blades have separate wooden roots, these can be glued in place now. Make sure that you fit them the right way round by checking their fit on the blade profile – the outer flat surfaces must be parallel. Don't use much glue because the roots must fit tightly to the blades or else the whole assembly will be too thick to fit in the blade holders. If the blades use plastic roots, these can be left until the covering has been fitted.

Covering the blades

Why bother? The covering does provide some protection, particularly for wooden blades, and it is much easier to clean. Conversely, the covering can hide damage and should always be removed for a check if you think that there is any chance of it. I was interested to discover a couple of years ago that I had orientation difficulty when flying a model, with plain white blades, at low level over snow. I realised just how much I watched the rotor disc when the model was below eye level and now I always try for some contrasting colours, particularly in winter when the light may be poorer. Seen in plan view, the area of the rotor disc is much larger than that of the fuselage, so it is worth making it as visible as possible.

There are two types of material which can be used for covering blades, heatshrink tubing and adhesive film. The adhesive film is supplied with the blades and can also be bought from a hardware shop. The heatshrink tubing is supplied with the blades and can also be bought from model shops (helicopter manufacturers supply it as a spare part) or from electronic component suppliers (check the required size before ordering). When buying heatshrink tubing, always get the smallest diameter which will do the job – the available shrinkage is quite spectacular but the film can shrink unevenly if there is a lot of slack to start with and this shows up as patchy colouring with the translucent varieties.

Tail blades can be covered in the same ways as main blades but I don't usually bother to balance them unless the helicopter has an unexplained vibration.

Using heatshrink tubing

I always use heatshrink tubing to cover blades, unless the section is reflex (i.e. it has a concave area) in which case I use adhesive film – the heatshrink would not follow the profile of the concave blade.

I use a heat gun to shrink the tubing and I think that you would find it difficult to do it any other way – with practice, it is possible to shrink the tube round the curved tips of blades but I wouldn't even try it using just an iron. Steam will shrink the tubing but you will need to ensure that the blade does not get wet if it is wood, and you will also need to take care to avoid scalding yourself. The first thing to do is to cut a length of tubing at least four inches longer than the blade (with practice, you will need less but if you don't allow enough, you will have wasted the whole length). Slide the blade into the tube, then take the heat gun and shrink one end of the tube so that it grips the end of the blade and cannot slide inwards. Next, shrink the other end of the tube so that it also grips the blade and, again, cannot slide inwards. Now use the gun to shrink the tubing as evenly as possible, working from one end of the blade towards the other until the whole blade is tightly covered. When you are satisfied, take a sharp scalpel and a ruler and *very carefully* cut just through the tubing, right round the blade, so that you can pull the scrap ends of tubing off the blade. You should allow the tubing to extend at least an inch past the point where the blade starts to taper at the root – this prevents the tubing from sliding off the blade under flying loads. I shrink the tubing and cut it as close to the root of the blade as possible – if the blades have wooden roots, you can take the covering right over the roots, provided that it doesn't make the blades too tight in the blade holders.

When you want to cover difficult tapers or curved blade ends, the trick is to pull and twist the tubing while shrinking it. Clamp the end of the tubing in a vice and then pull and twist the blade while applying heat – if you stop the tubing from contracting in one axis, it will contract more in the other axis. This does take practice and it is easy to apply too much heat and melt the tubing but it is surprising how neat the final result can be when you do master it. A few drops of thin cyano on the outer ends of wooden blades toughens the balsa against minor knocks, whichever type of covering you may be using.

Using adhesive film

When I use black carbon fibre blades which have a convex rear section, I cover them with the white adhesive film which is supplied with them. The one thing to avoid at all costs is having the film fold over so that two sticky sides meet – it is virtually impossible to separate them again. The only advice I can offer is to take it slowly and smooth out the film as you go, to avoid air bubbles – if you do get any, they can be pricked with a pin when you have finished. Working in a warm room also makes the job easier because the film is more flexible. There isn't any need to overlap the film because it sticks well to the composite blades – just trim it off at the trailing edge.

Adhesive film is suitable for covering wooden blades but you should overlap the join by at least ¼", because the film doesn't stick all that well to the balsa and the overlap will ensure that it doesn't peel off. The tidiest way to arrange the overlap is to start by applying the film to the underside of the blade at the rear, then go round the back edge of the blade, forward across the top, round the front edge, and back along the bottom, overlapping at the trailing edge. This hides the overlap and ensures that the airflow does not try to lift the edge and peel back the film.

Balancing the blades

There are two parts to this. First, you want to get the blades to the same weight and secondly, you want to achieve the same centre of gravity along the length. Unlike a fixed-wing model, you don't bother with the chordwise C of G, although its position does have a significant effect on the handling of some models – however, you can leave that to the designer and manufacturer of the blades.

To balance the blades you stick a piece of trim tape to the lighter blade. If you are using the seesaw, you will soon discover by experience just how much tape is necessary.

Equalising the weights

For this you need either a precision balance, so that you can weigh each blade separately, or a seesaw so that you can add weight to the lighter blade until the seesaw is level. The second option is the easier unless you have access to a suitable balance – you don't need to know the actual weight of the blade. When the seesaw is level, you will have a piece of trim tape which represents the difference in weight between the blades.

Equalising the centres of gravity

For this you bolt the blades together in the same alignment as they would have when fitted to the helicopter, and then you balance the assembly using the bolt as the pivot. You move the piece of trim tape along the lighter blade until the whole assembly hangs level and you then secure the tape in place.

Tracking tape

When you have finished balancing the blades, you should cut two equal pieces of tape of contrasting colours and apply one piece to the end of each of the blades. When the helicopter is hovered, it will be possible to see if one blade is higher than the other and to distinguish between them. The helicopter can then be landed and the linkages adjusted until the blades are in track together. It is also useful to mark the blade holders with the same colours as you have used for the tracking tape, so that you can remove the blades and then replace them again the same way round. You may find, particularly with wooden blades, that they run out of track if they are swapped over in the blade holders and marking the holders will avoid this inconvenience. Composite blades are usually so closely matched that they don't suffer from this, but wooden blades, being made from a natural material, will never be identical in their behaviour under flight loads.

Building and using a home-made seesaw balancer

Construction

I built this device many years ago from a description which someone gave me. I believe it was published but I can find no trace of it so I apologise to the originator for being unable to credit him for his design. The materials for the base are softwood from a DIY shop and ³⁄₃₂" piano wire (the base of mine is actually a bit of 15 mm ply). The seesaw uses 2" × ½" hardwood for the main piece and ½" × ¼" hardwood for the cross pieces. All the piano wire is simply epoxied in place. You can adjust the dimensions to suit but I would not reduce the height of the base because the trailing edge of one blade has to fit inside it when you do the C of G (the other one points upwards). The distance of the cross pieces from the centre wire of the seesaw **must** be equal, it is not enough just to make the seesaw balance. When you have finished the construction, place the seesaw on the base and sand the heavier end to balance it – since it is wood, it is likely that the density may vary so that it does not balance initially, but this can be adjusted. The critical parts are that the dimensions on each side are equal and that the seesaw sits level when empty.

Using the balancer

The balancer is designed to do both the weight and the C of G. The blades are first placed on the seesaw section, at right angles to the long axis and with the leading edges butted up to the cross pieces. This negates any effect of

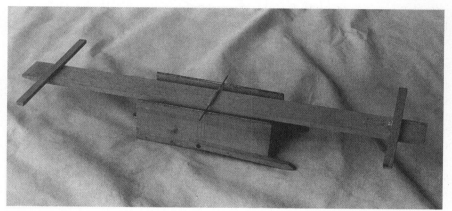

Figure 7.2 *My home-made seesaw balancer.*

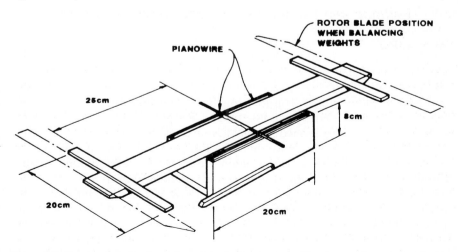

Figure 7.3 *Construction details and using the balancer to equalise the weights.*

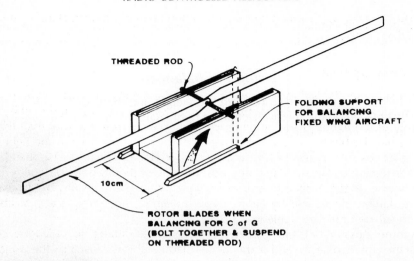

THREADED ROD

FOLDING SUPPORT
FOR BALANCING
FIXED WING AIRCRAFT

10cm

ROTOR BLADES WHEN
BALANCING FOR C of G
(BOLT TOGETHER & SUSPEND
ON THREADED ROD)

Figure 7.4 *Using the balancer to adjust the centre of gravity.*

differing spanwise C of G (although differing chordwise C of G would have
a minimal effect, which is ignored). You now note which is the higher blade,
make an inspired guess at how much trim tape you need and, not forgetting
to remove the backing paper, place it along the higher blade. Keep adjusting
the amount of tape, bearing in mind that you want to finish up with a strip
which can be wrapped round the blade and overlapped to prevent it from
peeling off in flight (I start with a strip about 1 cm longer than the circum-
ference of the blade and then adjust its width).

When you have finally persuaded the seesaw to stay level, remove the
tape and the blades, and the seesaw section. You will now need a length of
threaded rod at least 2 cm longer than the width of the base of the balancer
and of a diameter which will go through the bolt holes in the roots of the
blades. Thread the blades on to the rod and fit a nut either side of the blades,
so that they can be positioned parallel to one another and tightened together.
They should remain like that when the rod is laid across the base of the
balancer. A small piece of double-sided sticky tape (or servo mounting tape)
can be trapped between the blades to prevent them from moving. Now put
the balancing tape on the lighter blade and move it in or out until the blades
balance horizontally, then wrap the tape permanently round the blade at that
position. You now have a pair of blades which weigh the same and whose
C of G is in the same position, which is a good start when it comes to
reducing vibration.

You can now apply equal amounts of differently coloured tracking tape to the blade ends.

The awkward ones

The first possibility is that you have balanced the weights, but when you bolt the blades together, the heavy blade rises – this is caused by the centre of gravity of the lighter blade being much further away from the root than that of the heavier blade. Put the balancing tape as close to the root of the lighter blade as possible. Now cut two more pieces of tape of equal size (so that the blades remain of equal weight) and position one of them on the outer end of the heavier blade. If this doesn't make the heavier blade go down, cut two more, larger, pieces and try again. Next, adjust the remaining piece on the lighter blade until you achieve a balance.

Another possibility is that you cannot persuade the blades to sit level even with the tape right at the end of the lighter blade – this is caused by the centre of gravity of the heavier blade being much further away from the root than that of the lighter blade. The cure is the same as above, but you start with the additional tape at the outer end of the lighter blade instead of the heavier.

The third, and easiest, oddity is the pair of blades which are the same weight

Figure 7.5 A commercial balancer.

but do not balance. Again two equal pieces of tape are the cure, with the first piece at the outer end of the higher blade and the second piece as required to level the blades.

Looking after the blades

It is a good idea to check main and tail blades regularly for damage or any sign of the covering starting to depart. So, finally, a few words about what to do if you damage a main blade.

Never try to repair glass or carbon fibre blades, it is too dangerous. The hardwood section of a wooden blade is what carries the flight loads and the blade must be scrapped if that is damaged. Minor damage to the balsa section may be carefully repaired, but only if you are sure that there is no further damage – you may need to re-balance the blades afterwards. Quite apart from the immediate danger, if a main blade does shed bits in the air, the subsequent out-of-balance forces will probably destroy the helicopter even if there is enough blade left to fly it. Always check the blade root and the area of the bolt hole if you have any doubts about blade integrity. It is worth noting that the flight load being applied to the bolt which holds the blade in place is over 100 kg, even on a 30-size helicopter with a rotor speed of 1600 rpm – if you lose or damage the original bolt, make sure that any replacement is to the same specification, and do change the nyloc nuts if they lose their grip. If the wooden, or composite, blades have metal inserts at the bolt holes, they're not for decoration so don't be tempted to leave them out.

With care, a good pair of main blades will last for years – that makes it worthwhile getting them right in the beginning.

CHAPTER 8

Finding your own flying site

If you haven't found a club to join, you will need to arrange your own flying site. What should you be looking for?

Theoretically you may fly a radio controlled model on any public site unless it is specifically banned. In practice, model flying is usually specifically banned or restricted at public sites, and you should look for any relevant notices. The other alternative is to find a friendly farmer and ask if you can use one of his fields (or buy your own – a field, I mean, but a farm might be better!)

Whenever and wherever you are flying your model, you are subject to Article 56 of the Air Navigation Order, which says "A person shall not recklessly or negligently cause or permit an aircraft to endanger any person or property". If you do manage to find a private flying site, the responsibility for safe flying rests entirely with you, so I will list a few points which you should take into consideration. The other aspect to be considered is the noise of the model and the resulting annoyance to neighbours, and the comments below will also help to minimise this problem.

Radio interference

Modern radio transmitters have a maximum theoretical range of about one mile, which means that model flying sites should be a minimum of two miles apart. This means that you should make every effort to discover if there is any club flying in the area which might result in interference. If you do discover one, first, see if you can join it but, if you can't, tell them where you want to fly and make the necessary arrangements for times and radio frequencies so that you do not cause problems for one another.

Other possible theoretical sources of radio interference are hospitals and factories where high power paging systems are in use, although I must admit that I have never heard of these being a problem in practice.

What to avoid

Your take-off and landing point should be at least five hundred metres from any noise sensitive premises, and you should also avoid flying within two hundred metres of them, which obviously includes any houses, unless you have the owners' agreement. You shouldn't fly over roads, railway lines, car parks or other similar hazards and you should be able to park your own car where there is no danger of it being hit.

You need to keep well clear of such obstacles as telephone wires and electricity cables, particularly the high voltage ones on pylons. Those small cables which you often see on wooden poles in rural areas may well be carrying 12,000 volts and the ones on steel pylons carry several hundred thousand.

Other people . . .

Even if the site is private, you should consider the possibility of other people arriving to watch you flying, particularly if there is a public footpath nearby. If this does happen, their safety is your responsibility. You need to be particularly careful if there is any possibility of children being in the vicinity. Remember, when you are first learning you will have no time to glance around while you are flying to make sure that no-one has walked up behind you. Many members of the public with no experience of models will have absolutely no idea of the serious injury which can be caused if they are hit by one.

Obviously, this can be a particular problem if you are learning to fly on one of the sites which are open to the non-modelling public and it would be sensible to take someone along with you so that you can concentrate on learning to fly the helicopter.

. . . and animals

Farm and domestic animals seem to be little bothered by model aircraft and can sometimes be a nuisance because they are too inquisitive. Wildlife, too, seems not to be noticeably affected, however, common sense would dictate that you should never deliberately fly close to any animals or birds.

Full-size airfields

If you have one locally, the first thing to do is to find out when it is open and ask if you can fly there when it isn't. Airfields obviously make excellent model flying sites and there are a few around which even co-ordinate model and full-size flying simultaneously, although this does require very careful management.

If you simply want to fly near an airfield, there is no reason why you shouldn't providing you avoid any conflict with the full-size aircraft. The best plan is to visit the airfield and tell them what you plan to do. They, in turn, will explain what their requirements are and you should be able to reach a satisfactory arrangement.

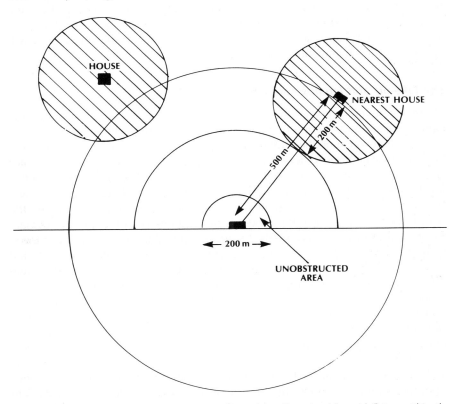

Figure 8.1 *Flying site. These are minimum dimensions. You should avoid flying within the 200 m circles around noise sensitive premises.*

The flying area

When you have found a suitable place, taking all the above points into consideration, you will need a flat mown area of grass at least ten metres square, but with no obstructions within at least one hundred metres in an arc of one hundred and eighty degrees. At first you will only need the ten-metre square

CHAPTER 9

Accessories and training aids

The accessories you need for flying the model and the others which could be helpful, including training undercarriages, buddy boxes and simulators

With the model is all ready to fly, there are a few accessories which you will need in order to go and fly it. Here they are (in no particular order of importance):

1 Fuel.
2 Fuelling system.
3 Power supply for the glow plug, a spare glow plug and a plug spanner.
4 Starter.
5 Power supply for the starter.
6 Something to carry it all in.

Fuel

In the absence of any advice from the engine manufacturer, I suggest that you buy a gallon of castor-based fuel containing 5 per cent nitromethane. For more information and recommendations, please read Chapter 5, *All about engines*

Fuel pumps

Having decided on your fuel, you now have to get it into the fuel tank. The cheapest method is to use a plastic squeeze bottle with a bit of fuel pipe pushed over the top and a piece of tube in the other end to connect it to the filler pipe. This may work but there are better (and cleaner) ways of doing the job.

What you need is a purpose-made pump which will both fill and empty the tank. It has to be purpose-made because the insides of the pump must be fuel-resistant. Hand pumps operate in either direction so can be used both to fill and to empty the model's fuel tank (which you should do at the end of every flying session). You can buy the geared variety but they tend to need priming, particularly when they get older. The best hand pump uses a flexible tube and a pair of rollers, which squeeze the tube and push a quantity of fuel along it as you turn the handle. The fuel does not contact any of the moving parts, the whole system is completely sealed, and there is no difference between filling and emptying.

You will also need a suitable length of silicone fuel tubing (similar to the type supplied with the helicopter fuel tank, and available in metre lengths from your model shop) and some metal tubing for connecting up when refuelling.

Filtering the fuel

Fuel filters are essential. You should filter the fuel as it comes out of the pump and you should also fit another filter in the model, between the tank and the carburettor. This is to make sure that only clean fuel reaches the carburettor, because it takes only a tiny piece of dirt to block the fuel jet, which will either stop the engine or at least cause it to run rough. Dirt is also one of the commonest reasons for the motor refusing to start in the first place.

In Chapter 10, *Building the model*, I have suggested that the simplest tank installations use only two pipes, one leading to the carburettor while the other goes to the exhaust nipple. This provides positive pressure to the tank and gives more consistent running but it means that the tank has to be filled though the carburettor feed. This must be done on the tank side of the filter so that any dirt which may be introduced ends up in the tank and is then filtered out before getting to the carburettor. If you fill the tank through the filter then any dirt caught during filling will be carried straight into the carburettor as soon as you start the motor.

Fuel filters need regular cleaning by flushing them with fuel in the opposite direction to the one in which they normally operate. This simply means removing the filter and pumping fuel backwards through it, thereby flushing out any debris. If you use the type of filter which unscrews, check the mesh insert for dirt.

Glow plugs, power supplies, and plug spanners

I dealt with the choice of glow plugs and their power supply in Chapter 5, *All about engines*. You will need a spanner to fit and remove the plug and the type of spanner depends on how easy it is to reach the plug when the motor is installed in the model. You may find that the cross-shaped spanner, which I have recommended in Chapter 10, will fit – the alternatives are a very short box-spanner which will fit within the cooling duct, or a very long box-

Figure 9.1 *Plug spanners – the one on the right uses a one-way bearing instead of a ratchet.*

spanner which will pass through the radio installation and the cooling duct. It is sometimes possible to use a ring-spanner if the clearance between the cylinder head cooling fins and the plug is sufficient. When removing the plug, you should note that there is a copper washer fitted between the plug and the cylinder head and that a new washer is supplied with the new plug.

In order to start the motor, you need to apply a voltage to the glow plug, which will make the coil heat up and provide the necessary ignition source – once the motor is running, there is sufficient heat generated by the combustion process to keep the coil hot enough to provide further ignition.

Depending on the manufacturer, the voltage required for glow plugs is either 1.2V, 1.5V or 2.0V (to be strictly accurate, glow plugs are designed to reach the correct heat when a particular current flows through the coil, and the quoted voltage of the plug makes certain assumptions about the resistance of the plug lead and the internal resistance of the power supply). Most plugs nowadays seem to be 1.5V.

A rechargeable battery is desirable, of which the most common are lead-acid accumulators or nickel cadmium cells. The lead-acid accumulator provides 2 volts which is too much for a 1.2V or 1.5V plug, but if you use a connecting lead of lighting flex about three feet in length, the extra resistance of the lead will reduce the current through the plug to an acceptable figure. The advantage of this type of cell is that it has a high capacity. Nicad cells provide only 1.2 volts (but they have a very low internal resistance) and they should be used with a short lead to compensate for the low voltage. The 1700mAh cells are of lower capacity than lead-acid batteries so should be regularly charged. An ammeter in the plug circuit enables you to check that the plug is working satisfactorily and shows up a short circuit or a failed plug element.

Glow connectors

Having chosen your glow battery, you will need a method of connecting it to the glow plug and the way this is done depends on how easy it is to reach the plug when the motor is installed in the model. Some models have the cylinder head tucked away inside the cooling duct while others are easily accessible.

The simplest way of connecting the plug to its power supply is to use a lead with two crocodile clips on the motor end (it does not matter which way round you connect the plug). One clip goes on the centre post of the plug and the other clip goes on one of the engine mounting bolts (or any other metal component which is connected to the body of the motor).

If the plug is inaccessible, you will need a remote glow connector. All this needs to be is an extension lead connected to the centre post of the plug, whose other end is accessible from outside the model – again, the other lead is clipped to a suitable bolt. If access to the interior is a problem, an external socket is the neatest solution and for this you will need a small plug and socket (phono plugs and sockets work very well). The socket is mounted in a convenient place on the model with the centre pin connected to the glow plug post using an extension lead and a miniature crocodile clip. The outer part of the plug is then connected to the engine mounting bolt as before.

There are several self-contained units available, which combine the power supply and the clip and, while they do make life easier, not all are suitable for helicopters. One type, which I use and which works well, consists of a combined battery, 12 volt charger and built-in ammeter, complete with a lead

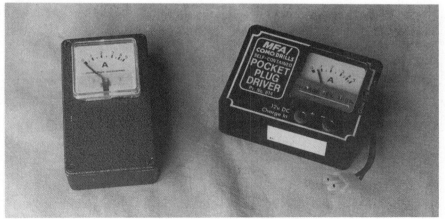

Figure 9.2 *Two power supplies for glow plugs. The ammeters are very useful.*

and glow clip – it is charged by connecting it directly to a 12V battery for 2 hours.

Starters

Unlike fixed-wing models where you can use your finger (suitably protected) to start the motor, a starter is a must for a helicopter (unless you have a motor which is fitted with a recoil start). There are several starters on the market and they range in cost from around £25 upwards.

Most starters will suit almost all models, but do check that the one you have in mind is suitable for your model. If your model uses a starter belt, you need a starter with a vee-groove in the starter cup (the bit which spins), and the cup should be made of aluminium. If your model uses a starter cone, check that the cup on the starter is large enough to grip the cone sufficiently. Starters run in either direction by reversing the battery connections, but if you buy a starter which is fitted with a one-way bearing (which allows the motor to accelerate without driving the starter, making it easier to tell when the motor has started), make sure that the one-way bearing operates in the correct sense. Reversing the battery connections is a waste of time in this case and two versions of these starters are available, for clockwise or anti-clockwise rotation. (Just in case you are wondering, all glow motors run in the same direction – anti-clockwise when seen from in front of the crankshaft, but the starter direction

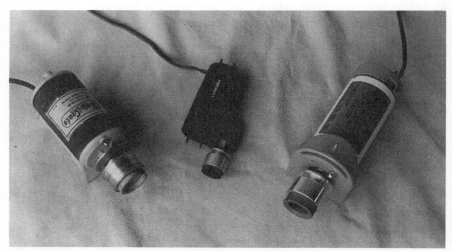

Figure 9.3 *The starter in the middle uses a one-way bearing to allow the engine to accelerate. The one on the right can be run on 24V for much larger engines.*

depends which end of the crankshaft you use to start them.)

There is a rechargeable, self-contained, nicad-powered starter on the market but it is very expensive and I have no experience of using it with a helicopter.

Power panels

A power panel is a device which combines starter socket, adjustable glow plug supply, fuel pump switch and fuel pump in one box (although not all panels contain a fuel pump). The panel may be literally a panel, with the components exposed at the rear, or it may be contained in a box with the necessary connections on the outside. There is an input lead, which is connected to a separate 12V battery.

At first sight, power panels are convenient but you may have a problem if you need to replace individual components (such as a fuel pump). Check that the leads which connect the panel to the 12V battery are adequate – they should be at least as substantial as your starter leads if you are going to plug the starter into the panel. You need to ensure that the 12V battery is kept well charged, otherwise the glow voltage may fall when the starter is used.

Batteries and chargers

Whether you have decided on a power panel or separate components, at the very least you will need a 12V battery to power the starter.

There are two alternative sources, the local motorbike shop or the model shop. Your model shop should be able to supply a rechargeable 12-volt sealed lead-acid battery of about 6 amp-hour capacity (or more) and this will be adequate. It will be spill-proof, maintenance-free and reasonably compact – don't forget, you are going to have to carry all these accessories as well as the helicopter. You will need a 12 volt charger and your model shop will be able to advise you. Don't forget to take the usual precautions when charging sealed cells – they give off hydrogen gas, which is inflammable, in just the same way as the traditional wet cells.

Finally, something in which to carry it all

You will soon hear the words 'pit box' which is the modeller's term for 'something to carry it all in'. Don't buy anything until you have seen what other people use and, more to the point, you have decided what you need to carry and can check that it will all fit. I use a large aluminium camera case, which is big enough to contain half a gallon of fuel as well as my transmitter, starter, 12V battery and so on and, yes, it is heavy but it has a shoulder strap which leaves both hands free for carrying helicopters. Camera accessory shops are expensive but model shops often seem to have these cases at reasonable prices, or you may see them advertised in the modelling magazines.

If the list looks daunting, you may well be able to borrow some of the equipment from fellow club members for a while, and this will give you a chance to see some of the different options which are available. As usual, buy the best you can afford and treat second-hand equipment with suspicion unless you know its history. Incidentally, years of experience have left me convinced that the simplest devices are the best, so I recommend a mechanical fuel pump, a glow battery, and a 12 volt starter with a separate battery.

Other useful accessories

These are certainly not necessary but they can save time, and (occasionally) money if they detect a potential problem before it actually happens. Many are devoted to monitoring the health of the radio batteries, which are the commonest source of modellers' problems.

Multi-chargers and fast chargers

The ideal charger, which will meet all your requirements for many years, is one of the mains multi-chargers. They have a selection of constant-current outputs and will charge radio nicad packs and 2V, 6V and 12V lead-acid batteries (automatically in some cases), at the same time. They cost from about

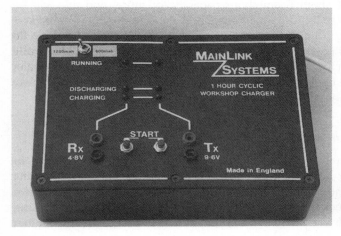

Figure 9.4 *Mains workshop fast charger/cycler for when you forget to charge the night before.*

£30 upwards but one will replace all your other chargers and provide much greater flexibility.

Fast chargers are useful if you have forgotten to charge your model in time to go flying. Most fast chargers use a technique called **delta-peak** which enables them to detect when the nicad is fully charged and then either to cut out or to drop to a trickle charge. Typical charge rates are 200 – 600mA and a partly charged receiver pack can often be topped up in one to two hours, while you have breakfast. Delta-peak chargers can be fooled by nicads which are in poor condition, so a cycler is also useful if you use this type of charger.

Battery monitors

The commonest type of battery monitor is a small device which is carried on the helicopter and which indicates the receiver battery state. It has coloured LEDs which, in the simplest form, show green for go and red for stop. The monitor is connected to the receiver and senses the nicad voltage when everything is operating.

Glitch counters

These are also connected to the receiver, and may be combined with a battery monitor. The glitch counter checks the behaviour of the receiver and senses if it is receiving interference, which may be the result of transmitter problems or radio interference, or may be caused by the vibration of loose or broken

Figure 9.5 On the right is a glitch counter and on the left a combined glitch counter and battery monitor, for installation in the helicopter.

metal components on the helicopter. The glitch counter will include some form of display to show how many times interference has occurred.

Battery checkers

These are small expanded-scale voltmeters which also incorporate an electrical load. When the nicad is plugged into the checker, the voltmeter will indicate its charge state. Unfortunately, because of the discharge characteristics of nicads, the reading will be constant anywhere between 90% and 10% charged. This limits the usefulness of these devices mainly to identifying the cause of a crash or radio failure.

Figure 9.6 *This battery checker has sockets for receiver and transmitter nicads.*

Battery cyclers

These are chargers which fully discharge the nicad before starting the charge. Nicads can suffer a loss of capacity if they are regularly charged without being fully discharged – this is called the memory effect – and a cycler can be useful because it eliminates this. Some cyclers include a display which shows the capacity of the nicad when it has been discharged. If you fully charge the nicad, then cycle it, the reading will show if the capacity of the nicad has fallen off, in which case you should repeat the cycle. If the capacity is still below its specification after several cycles, you should replace the nicad.

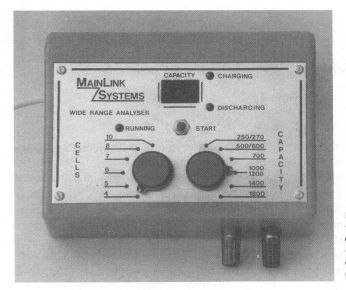

Figure 9.7 *Battery cycler with a capacity read-out – it can analyse 4–10 cell nicad packs of up to 1,800 mAh capacity.*

Pitch gauges

These are used for adjusting the pitch of the main rotor blades. They are clamped to the blade being checked, levelled against the flybar, and the pitch angle is then read directly off the gauge. They are only accurate when used on symmetrical blades, although they can be used for comparing pitch settings for similar blades when fitted to different helicopters. They are no substitute for test flying and are not necessary for setting up a helicopter.

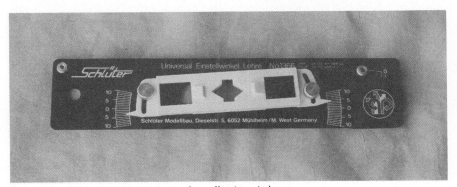

Figure 9.8 *Pitch gauge for setting up the collective pitch range.*

Dial gauges

These are useful for accurate alignment of the clutch and flywheel. This is not a problem with most thirty-size helicopters but there are notorious exceptions among the larger competition-oriented machines, where the use of a dial gauge is mandatory.

Head loaders

These are a good solution to the problem of setting the mixture with the engine running at full throttle. The main blades are removed and replaced with the head loaders, using the same bolts and tightening them to the same degree. When the engine is started, the large plastic balls on the arms will provide a similar amount of aerodynamic drag to that produced by a pair of main blades and you will be able to apply full power to check the carburettor main needle setting. One point to watch is that the torque compensation will apply tail pitch as you open the throttle, so the tail may try to swing (although, with the model on grass, I haven't found this to be a problem). I recommend that you start the engine, carry the helicopter to a safe area, stand behind the model and then apply power, using the rudder if necessary. It is much safer to close the throttle again, before attempting to adjust the mixture.

Figure 9.9 My Star 30 fitted with head loaders for setting up the engine.

Head loaders are also useful for running in a new engine but it is possible that the absence of airflow might make the engine run slightly hotter. However, this should simply mean that you finish up with a slightly rich main needle setting, which is not going to cause any damage. Head loaders are available in two different sizes for different engine capacities (thirty or sixty).

Training undercarriages, buddy boxes and simulators

One of the advantages of learning to fly helicopters instead of fixed-wing models is that you start literally from the ground up, whereas with a fixed-wing model someone else has to do the take-off and landing for you. Furthermore, you can take things at your own speed and you are not dependent on having assistance throughout the early stages.

However, there are one or two items which can save you from trouble, particularly at first, and a good simulator can be invaluable throughout your flying career.

Training aids

Training undercarriages

These include hoops, crossed sticks and floats, and are intended to reduce the risk of the helicopter tipping over. The purpose of all of them is to increase the effective size of the undercarriage so that the helicopter can be tipped much further from the horizontal before the main rotor touches the ground. They are also useful for preventing a roll-over when the machine is landed while travelling sideways.

Hoops and crossed sticks are the more effective devices, floats help to prevent the skids from digging in but are often not strong enough to resist bending in a firm landing.

Commercial versions are available but if you decide to make your own, you will need two garden canes (the plastic versions are OK), suitable wire or plastic ties, and either a plastic hoop or four plastic balls (practice golf balls will do but something larger is better). The canes will need to be about twice the length of the model's undercarriage skids and they should be joined in the middle in the shape of a cross. The hoop is then attached to the outer ends of the canes from below, and the assembly is then attached to the underside of the helicopter's skids. The canes should be at forty-five degrees to the skids and the centre of the cross should be directly under the main mast of the helicopter, so that the centre of gravity is not affected. If you choose to use

Figure 9.10 *A commercial training undercarriage using four plastic balls instead of a hoop.*

four balls instead of a hoop, their purpose is to prevent the ends from digging into the ground or catching in the grass and they should be firmly fixed to the ends of the canes.

The whole assembly must be secure because, if it comes loose, it may cause precisely the sort of accident which it is intended to prevent.

This type of aid is undoubtedly of value when you are first starting to hover. However (and this may be of interest to whoever you ask to set up your machine), this type of device needs to be flexible and it can start to vibrate if the model is being flown around. I have had to land a model because the vibration became so severe that controlling the model became a problem.

Other devices

There have been various training systems which enabled the beginner to mount his machine on some sort of gimballed arm. This then allowed him to fly the helicopter within its limited range of travel. I do not know of anything available at present, but, in order for it to be successful, it would need to be both large and expensive and I would question the need.

At the other extreme, there was a fashion at one time for persuading one's 'helper' to restrain the tail with a piece of string while the novice hovered the helicopter, all the time keeping down elevator applied in order to keep the string tight. Realisation of the accident potential has recently ensured a rapidly diminishing supply of 'helpers'!

With the exception of the training undercarriage, there is no need for further aids nowadays. Modern gyros and helicopters are so stable and predictable that most people rapidly master the basic flying skills – the only real requirements are patience, persistence and practice (and someone to set up your model).

Buddy boxes

This curious expression refers to the linking of two transmitters so that the beginner can fly with a type of dual control. While the instructor holds up a sprung switch on his transmitter, the student has control but, as soon as the instructor releases the switch, control reverts to the instructor. Variations on the sophistication of the system may allow the instructor to retain control of one or more channels throughout the exercise, so that the student can learn the effect of each of the controls independently.

Obviously, the transmitters have to be compatible for this system to work, and this means that they have to be of the same make. Furthermore, not all of a manufacturer's transmitters are necessarily equipped with this facility and those which are may only be suitable for use in the slave (student) role. This

Figure 9.11 *For the helicopter that has everything – a waterproof cover.*

radio when flying both the simulator and the model, simulators with transmitters cost nearly twice as much as those without.

The software

This varies and, while they are all good, the best is not necessarily the one with the prettiest models or the biggest mountains. As a rough guide, and assuming that you have the necessary computing power to take advantage of it, the program which requires the most powerful computer is likely to be the best buy. It will probably give you the most realistic models and will allow you to tailor them to fly like your own, even if they don't look particularly like it.

CHAPTER 10

Building the model

What you need and how to do it, including installing the engine, fuel system and radio

The amount of work that will be required will obviously depend on whether you are building from a kit or are just completing the assembly of an ARTF model. However, even with an ARTF model, you should still check that the assembly is correct and that all the nuts and bolts are tight.

You will need a reasonable amount of space in which to build the helicopter – I have a workbench eight feet long by four feet deep, but this is a luxury. I use a home-made stand about eighteen inches square to raise the helicopter off the bench by about five inches – I find this helps to keep the tail clear of the bench and I can keep the frequently used tools under the stand. Once you have fitted the tail boom, you will find that turning the helicopter round makes a good way of sweeping everything onto the floor and the stand does help to prevent this. Once run, helicopters do drip oil from the exhaust so you will need to protect the work surface if necessary.

The tools you will need (and the ones which are useful)

Model helicopter kits often include the tools which you will need, mainly because there are so few of them. All the kits and engines which I know of are metric, so you can forget anything else for now.

The essentials

The kit may use 3 mm (M3) and 4 mm (M4) cap head bolts, for which you will require Allen keys (these are also known as hexagonal wrenches and are usually included in the kit), and you will need a 5.5 mm spanner for M3 nuts and a 7 mm spanner for M4 nuts. Some kits also use M2.6 bolts and you will need a 5 mm spanner for their nuts.

For the engine, you will need an 8 mm spanner for the glow plug and a

10 mm one for the propeller nut. The simplest solution is to buy one of the cross-shaped purpose-made spanners, which has 8, 9, 10 and 12 mm sockets as well as threaded holes for spare plugs.

You will also need one large and one small cross-head screwdriver and probably a small flat screwdriver as well. Long-nose pliers are likely to be useful too. You will need to have a means of balancing the main rotor blades, unless you always use glass or carbon fibre ones – Chapter 7 tells you all about this.

Helicopters vibrate and the nuts and bolts tend to work loose. This problem is solved where possible by the use of nyloc nuts (the ones with plastic inserts) and you should never replace these with plain ones. However, there are places where this is not practical and these are where you will need to use some form of thread-locking liquid (often called 'Loctite' although, like 'Hoover', this is actually a brand name). Model shops stock various makes of these liquids but some of them are too strong for our use and they can make it very difficult to undo the bolts when you want to, even when used very sparingly. The simplest solution is to use liquid silicone, which you should be able to buy in a tube from your model shop, and this will also help to prevent screws from loosening where they are used straight into plastic. The other alternative is to buy one of the thread locks which are listed as low strength or serviceable.

The luxuries

Which you will regard as essential once you have used them. These include nut runners and ball-ended Allen keys (ball drivers) and the most valuable tool of all, a rechargeable electric screwdriver with a set of interchangeable bits (which include Allen keys, cross-head bits and socket spanners).

Also into this class comes a dial gauge for really accurate alignment of the flywheel and clutch, and a pitch gauge for setting up the main blades (although it will only be accurate if you use symmetrical blades and you will still need to fly the model for final adjustment). I use a dial gauge for every model I build and a pitch gauge once a year (if I am bored and can't think of anything else to do) – I think this is a measure of their relative importance. I don't want to overstress the need for a dial gauge because many helicopter fliers never use one, but if your model has an unexplained high frequency vibration or the fuel tends to foam in the tank, then it is worth checking the accuracy of the flywheel alignment (or asking someone else to do it). If it is impossible to align the clutch accurately, using a dial gauge, try changing the prop driver on the engine – assuming, of course, that the helicopter uses a prop driver!

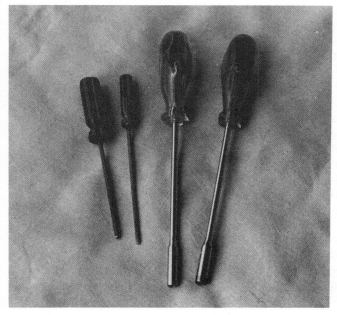

Figure 10.1 *Ball drivers and nut runners are always useful.*

Building the model

The amount of work will vary depending on whether you are building an ARTF model or a kit but the first thing to do is to read the instructions and to make sure that you have understood them – if something doesn't appear to make sense, ask the model shop or the distributors to explain. Always remember that the main rotor blades will be reaching four hundred miles an hour and the load on the bolts on which the main blades pivot can exceed fifty kilograms.

ARTF

Manufacturers' opinions of the meaning of the word 'almost' do seem to vary a bit but you will probably have to fit the undercarriage, radio, rotor head and main blades, and, possibly, the tail boom and engine. If you can still fit the engine with the undercarriage in place, the best order in which to work is usually to fit the undercarriage as soon as possible, because the helicopter will then stand on its skids while you work on it. If the tail boom is not already fitted, leave it until last because it is much easier to turn the model round without it. Finally, don't forget to check that the manufacturer has tightened everything up. I will go into more detail in the next section.

Building from a kit

When you open the box, you will usually find that the various components are in individual numbered bags. You should also find that the instructions tell you to open each bag and to use all the contents to build a particular sub-assembly, these sub-assemblies being joined later to complete the helicopter. The instructions should also have a page which describes all the various nuts, bolts, screws, washers and so on in detail and you will need to study this carefully as you proceed. Most kits nowadays contain exactly the right amount of all the components, so if you use an 8 mm bolt when you should have used a 6 mm one, you are likely to find that the 6 mm one which remains will be too short. It really is worth finding a ruler and measuring the various bolts so that you can be sure of using the correct ones. This also applies to using cap head or pan head bolts – never replace cap heads with pan heads because cap head bolts are normally stronger than pan heads. Always use nyloc nuts or locking washers wherever the instructions require them, and that applies to thread lock as well. The instructions may tell you to apply grease (which will be included in the kit) – if they don't, there is no need to do so.

Fitting the clutch and flywheel to the engine

Before bolting the engine in the model, you will have to fit the flywheel and clutch. If the helicopter uses the engine with the prop driver (the large aluminium disc with a knurled front face) in place, you will probably find that there are no alternative fittings for different engines. If, however, you are told to remove the prop driver, you may well have to fit one of a selection of adapters to the crankshaft before fitting the flywheel, each adapter being suitable for a particular engine.

If you do need to remove the prop driver, take care not to damage the engine in the process. If you are lucky and the prop driver has not been pulled tightly onto its split tapered collet, it will be possible to remove it by hand. However, if it is tight, the correct tool for the job is a small puller (OS make one which fits their engines) but you can use an aluminium plate with a slot in it which fits the groove in the prop driver. Support the plate and tap the end of the crankshaft with a wooden mallet to release the prop driver. You may find that the model shop will do this job for you if you ask them.

Check that you are using the correct adapter if necessary, then fit the flywheel and clutch shoes as instructed, checking the run-out with a dial gauge if you have one available (but don't worry if you haven't). If the shoes are plastic, make sure that the springs are fitted correctly. If the model uses a one-piece machined clutch shoe unit, you will find that the spring section is comparatively soft. Helicopter clutch shoes only move a very small amount when engaging and there is no need for much spring action. The clutch is not designed to slip once engaged and you will find that the wear on the lining is negligible under normal operating conditions. Now is probably a good time to check that the clutch lining has been glued into the clutch bell and not merely pushed in as a convenient means of packing it. If the lining needs to be glued, use a very thin smear of epoxy and press the lining firmly into place.

I normally use liquid silicone to secure the crankshaft nut and the bolts which retain the clutch shoes, the only exception being when locking washers are provided.

Installing the engine

Before you bolt the engine in the model, look at the carburettor and note which way the arm moves to open and close the throttle. Make a note of this because you will need to check that the throttle servo is working in the correct direction and you will not be able to see the carburettor once the engine is installed. Starting the engine with full power selected is not only bad for the clutch, it can seriously affect either your health or your wealth or both.

The engine is bolted into the engine mount, again using liquid silicone, and the engine mount is bolted into the sideframes of the helicopter. Before fitting the engine, check that the throttle will close completely (see Chapter 5) and that

Figure 10.2 *Use a very thin layer of epoxy to secure the clutch lining. The one-way bearing for the top start is just visible in the centre of the clutch shoes.*

the carburettor mounting to the engine is secure – if screws are used, apply some thread lock to prevent them from working loose. Now is the time to fit the throttle extension arm if necessary and, if you are using a ball link on the throttle, now is also the time to fit the ball to the arm and to fit the glow plug.

The engine should be aligned according to the instructions. If there is a top start, check that the starter socket is free to rotate backwards – this ensures that the shaft is correctly lined up with the one-way bearing in the centre of the clutch shoes. When the engine is running, you should be able to prevent the starter socket from turning with one finger. If you can't, the engine is out of alignment. Again, use liquid silicone to secure the mounting bolts.

If the helicopter uses a belt start, don't forget to fit the belt before installing the engine.

Assembling the frames

If you are putting screws into plastic, take care not to strip the threads, particularly if you are using machine threaded screws. If you do strip a thread, try applying *Pacer Zaplock* to the screw before you put it in, then tighten it carefully and this will usually hold satisfactorily. If you have to screw grub screws into something like a plastic gear, it is very difficult to tell when the screw is tight. A drop of light oil will reduce the friction between the screw and the plastic, which should enable you to feel when the screw meets the shaft. If the grub screw is securing a plastic gear to a flat on the shaft, always line the flat up as accurately as possible. The grub screw will not pull the gear into alignment if the gear is tight on the shaft. Wherever plain nuts are fitted instead of nylocs, consider using thread lock or liquid silicone.

Follow the instructions for lining up any gears. If nothing is mentioned, feed a strip of newspaper between the gears to give a small clearance, then tighten up the mountings, before removing the paper. Turn the gears through several complete revolutions to check for any high spots, then adjust again if necessary. Always ensure that the maximum area of the two gears is in contact, to minimise the wear, and also check that bevel gears are correctly aligned at the appropriate angle. Don't apply grease to exposed gears unless the instructions tell you to and then only use the correct variety or it will be thrown everywhere when the gears turn. If there are any sealed gearboxes, check whether they should be packed with grease before final assembly.

The tail drive and gearbox

There are two types of tail drive, toothed belt and wire (or shaft). The tension

Figure 10.3 *The tail gearbox for a belt-driven My Star 30.*

of the toothed belt is adjusted by moving the tail boom in or out of the side-frames and the instructions should tell you how tight it should be. The usual guide is that you should just be able to push the inner faces of the belt together about an inch behind the front driving gear. Make sure that the necessary quarter twist is applied to the belt (not one and a quarter!) and that it is in the correct direction.

Wire drives are straightforward. They may include a sliding coupling so that you can remove the boom without undoing a grub screw – make sure that the correct gap is left between the end of the shaft and the inner face of the coupling. Also check that the supporting bearings are in the right places in the boom – the placing may be critical in order to prevent the shaft from whirling. If the couplings use grub screws, these should have thread lock applied to them to prevent them from loosening and don't be tempted to leave any out. If the shaft has flats on it, make sure they are lined up as instructed. Wire tail drives are very reliable and trouble free if you adjust them correctly to start with (and, contrary to any stories you may hear, wire tail drives do not suffer from wind-up, unlike some of the pilots who use them!)

The tail blades can usually be fitted with no further preparation, but do check that you fit them the right way round (the top blade **usually** moves backwards when the head is turning in the correct direction). You may notice

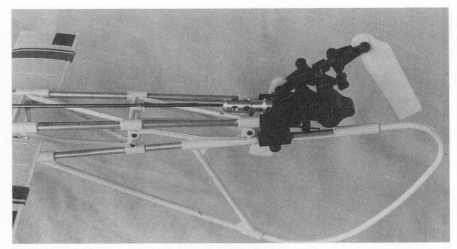

Figure 10.4 *The tail gearbox for a wire-driven Hirobo Lama.*

that the tail blades are not at zero pitch when the control arm on the tail gearbox is in its mid position. This is correct because the arm will be in the middle when the helicopter is in the hover but there must be sufficient tail pitch to oppose the torque at that time.

Fuel tanks

The helicopter kit will include the fuel tank, which will usually be designed specifically for that helicopter. The internal and external plumbing will be provided but you will probably have to fit it and the instructions may not be very helpful.

Helicopters operate most satisfactorily if you use exhaust pressure to pressurise the fuel tank and push the fuel to the carburettor. Since the fuel tube from the tank to the carburettor is easily accessible, that can be used for refuelling, so you will only need two tubes in all.

You will probably have to fit the metal pipes which pass through the bung in the neck of the tank and one of these should be curved through ninety degrees while the other should be straight. The curved pipe is positioned in the sealing bung so that the curved section of the pipe is inside the tank with its end just touching the top of the tank. The straight pipe is pushed through a convenient hole in the sealing bung. The clunk weight is fitted to the thin silicone tubing, which is then pushed onto the inner end of the straight pipe,

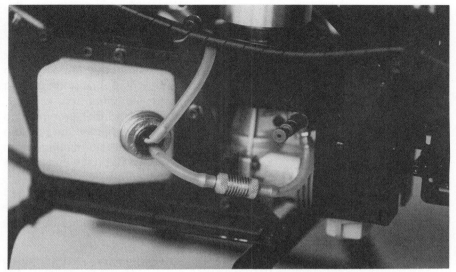

Figure 10.5 *Simple fuel tank installation. Refuelling is done by disconnecting the filter.*

and the bung is pushed into the tank. You should now hold up the tank to the light and check that the clunk weight is free to swing inside the tank without touching the opposite wall of the tank – the clearance should be about one-eighth of an inch and you should shorten the silicone tubing if necessary. This gap is vital because, if the clunk is too close to the tank wall when the engine draws fuel, the supply will be restricted and the engine will run erratically and may stop.

The tank is installed in the model and standard silicone fuel tubing is used to connect the curved pipe to the nipple on the muffler. The straight pipe, with the clunk on its other end, is connected to the carburettor. You should use an in-line fuel filter in this connection to the carburettor – to fill the fuel tank, the tube is pulled off the filter on the tank side and fuel is pumped into the tank. The curved pipe will now act as an overflow and any surplus fuel will flow into the muffler, whereas, when the engine is running, exhaust muffler pressure will pass in the opposite direction.

Fitting the cabin

If it is left to you to install the glazing, the best way of doing this is to bolt the body to the helicopter, then to trim the glazing down to size in very small steps, checking regularly how it is fitting. Don't rely on the lines which may be moulded in the glazing. If the glazing is shown as only being screwed in place, don't be tempted to use adhesive as well. If you do have to use adhesive, use masking tape to prevent it from spreading too far (unless you are using cyano) and try a test piece to see if liquid silicone will do the job – it often will, particularly if you roughen the surfaces, and it is probably the easiest adhesive with which to work, as well as being flexible when set.

The bolt holes in the canopy should be fitted with rubber grommets to protect the canopy against cracking and so that you can tighten the bolts up enough to prevent them from continually coming undone and falling out in flight. You may want to drill a hole for the receiver aerial, in which case this should be fitted with a rubber grommet as well.

I have avoided a blow by blow account of building the machine. Most modern kits have good instructions which should be followed in sequence but, if you do have a problem, don't hesitate to ask the model shop or the distributor of the kit.

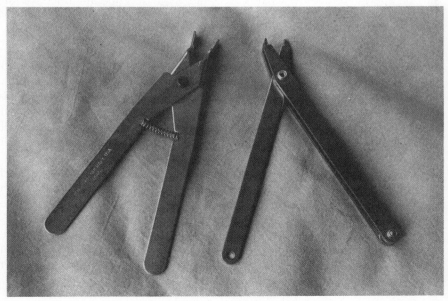

Figure 10.6 *These special pliers are used for undoing ball joints.*

CHAPTER 11

Installing the radio

What the transmitter functions do and how to install and connect the radio in the model

The functions and what they do

The transmitter will have various additional adjustments and options, such as **dual rate** and **travel adjust**, and these are called 'functions'. The descriptions that follow are generally valid for both conventional and computer radios. Not all of the following functions will be fitted to conventional transmitters but you may be interested to know what is available. I will describe the functions for a typical computer radio because these are more comprehensive, although they serve basically the same purpose whatever the transmitter.

Before starting to set any adjustments for the model, you should set all the controls to their normal positions. With a conventional transmitter, you should put all the switches to normal/forward and all the rotary pots to 100%. With a computer transmitter, you should do a RESET – the instructions will explain precisely how. Before going any further, if you have a computer radio, you don't need to know anything about computers. The programs are simply lists of functions and are generally self-evident, but you should refer to the instructions if you are in doubt.

It is often useful to have the receiver switched on when adjusting the functions because you can then see the effect of any changes. However, care is obviously necessary when the engine is running (for instance, *do not* reverse the throttle servo – it is much safer not to reverse any servos with the engine running). I will continue to use the fixed-wing names for cyclic and tail rotor controls (elevator, aileron and rudder).

Dual rate may be available on elevator, aileron and rudder and it enables you to vary the amount of servo movement with stick movement for these three channels. The standard servo movement is 100% and the switch position can be set for any value between 0% and 125% – both switch positions may be adjustable. Dual rate limits the overall travel of the servo – if the normal servo travel is 80° (40° either side of neutral) when the stick is moved from one extreme to the other, the servo will move through 40° if you set dual rate

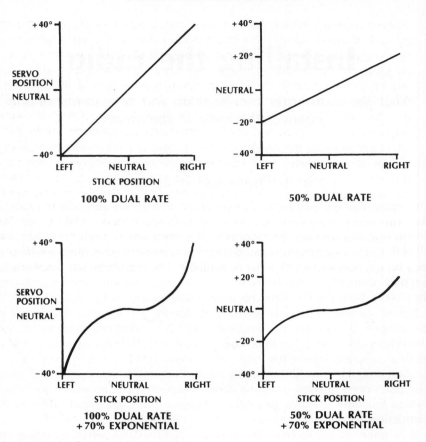

Figure 11.1 *Dual rate and exponential.*

to 50%. However, the movement will now be 20° either side of neutral. **Exponential** may be varied between −100% and +100% (the use of positive exponential reduces the stick sensitivity about the neutral, whereas negative exponential increases it, but neither affects the total available servo movement). Exponential settings are coupled with rate settings and are automatically selected at the same time. There may also be an additional option to have the dual rate and exponential settings selected automatically when you select either, or both, of the stunt (idle up) curves or throttle hold. The use of dual rate to reduce the servo movement will make the helicopter less responsive to the control inputs.

Servo reverse enables you to reverse the direction of the servo movement for each channel, for use where it is not possible to use the other side of the servo output device (as is often the case with helicopter installations). It is no longer normally possible to buy servos with different operating directions and this function has taken their place. Servo reverse should do just that – it should reverse the direction of operation of the servo which is plugged into the channel which you have reversed. It doesn't matter how that channel is operated, be it by its own control, as the slave in a mixer, or, for the tail rotor on a helicopter, by the revolution mixing (torque compensation), so if you use **rudder servo reverse**, the rudder servo will *always* operate in the opposite direction. The effect on the model should be the same as if you had removed the servo and replaced it with one which operated in the reverse direction.

Travel adjust enables you to select the desired amount of servo movement independently on either side of neutral. Standard travel is 100% and this can be adjusted between 0% and 150% for each side of each of the channels (if 80° is the normal servo movement, 150% on both sides gives a total of 120° of servo movement). You should note the difference between travel adjust and

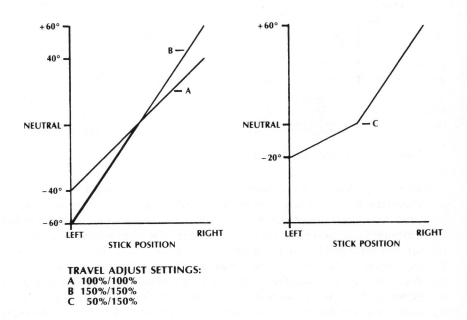

TRAVEL ADJUST SETTINGS:
A 100%/100%
B 150%/150%
C   50%/150%

Figure 11.2 *Travel adjustment.*

dual rate. The former allows you to set the servo movement independently on either side of neutral whereas the latter affects the overall servo movement but leaves it symmetrical on either side of neutral.

Throttle and collective pitch curves

The helicopter is always set up mechanically so that it hovers with the throttle stick in the mid position and the main rotor rpm at the correct value, this being achieved by adjusting the linkages in the helicopter. The throttle and collective servos are plugged into the appropriate outlets of the receiver and both servos will then operate when the throttle stick is moved. If you set the various transmitter adjustments to zero, the two servos will move through the same arc and their relative positions will be the same throughout that arc.

In the simplest system, the movement of the throttle servo is left unchanged but the relative position of the collective servo is altered so that the main rotor blade setting is always what is needed for the power which the engine is producing, whatever the throttle setting. However, this is actually achieved simply by limiting the amount of collective servo movement independently above and below the neutral (hover) point. This will ensure that the main rotor speed is satisfactory at full power, in the hover, and with the throttle closed, but it may well not be as required at any intermediate stick positions.

The computer transmitter has at least two throttle curves and two pitch curves, each of which allows you to set the servo positions at five or more points in the stick's range of movement. This means that the pitch can be matched much more accurately to the power output at any stick position. The first, or **normal**, pair of curves will be used for hovering the helicopter, where the main rotor speed will be set to around 1500 rpm for stability and smooth handling.

By increasing the throttle settings and/or reducing the pitch settings, the second pair of curves will be adjusted to increase the main rotor speed perhaps to 1800 rpm, which will give a more rapid control response for aerobatics. The minimum throttle setting in the throttle curve will be set higher so that the main rotor speed does not fall off when the throttle stick is pulled right back. Furthermore, the collective pitch setting will be reduced so that negative pitch is applied when the stick is pulled right back and this, with the increased throttle, will produce lift when the helicopter is inverted at the top of a loop, preventing gravity from exercising its usual influence. You will note that this is all achieved simply by selecting one switch to a different position, while the helicopter is in flight. More advanced transmitters may have five throttle curves and seven pitch curves.

Idle up

A basic helicopter transmitter will probably have a switch labelled *idle up* or something similar. What this does is to enable you to set a minimum setting below which the throttle will not close even though the throttle stick continues to be pulled back. This will prevent the main rotor speed from decreasing when the throttle stick is pulled back during aerobatics, but it has no effect on the collective pitch.

Throttle hold

The other switch which you may see will be labelled *hold*, or *throttle hold*, and this is used for practising autorotations. What throttle hold does is to disconnect the throttle channel from the collective and to leave the throttle stick controlling only the collective. The throttle servo moves to a pre-set position which leaves the engine running at a reliable idle. This means that the pilot can position the model somewhere overhead, then select throttle hold and practise an autorotation – if he decides that it is not working out, all he has to do is to switch throttle hold off and the engine will respond normally, enabling him to climb away and try again. There will be a means of adjusting the idling throttle setting, and the computer transmitter may have a separate pitch curve which is selected automatically when the throttle hold switch is moved. It is usual for the revolution mix to be switched off when hold is selected, and the rudder servo may be moved to a pre-set position. This is available so that the model is in trim if it is fitted with a slipper clutch and has a driven tail during autorotations.

Hover throttle and hover pitch

The transmitter may have two further rotary controls. The **hover throttle** control adjusts the throttle setting around the mid-stick position and the **hover pitch** control adjusts the collective setting at the same point. These can be used to alter the main rotor speed slightly when the model is in the hover, to suit the prevailing weather conditions. These controls do not affect the basic settings and they only have any effect when the throttle stick is close to the mid point.

Revolution mixing, or ATS

The engine of the helicopter drives two rotors. The result of the main rotor turning in one direction is that the fuselage tries to turn in the opposite direction, and this tendency is resisted by the tail rotor. As an aside, the tail rotor produces thrust which not only prevents the fuselage from turning but also tries to push the whole machine sideways – this is in turn opposed by a small application of aileron which makes the model lean sideways. The effect is often very noticeable when the helicopter is in the hover with the skids at eye level, when you will see that one skid is higher than the other.

The pitch of the tail rotor blades is varied by the rudder stick in order to prevent the fuselage from turning and to control the heading of the helicopter. However, every time that the power setting, and thereby the torque, is changed, the tail rotor setting needs to be changed in order to keep the helicopter's heading constant. The purpose of revolution (revo) mix is to do this for you.

The neutral point from which the revo mix is set up is the hover and at this point the mix output is zero. When the helicopter is in a stable hover, the control linkages are adjusted so that the rudder servo is at neutral and there is sufficient tail rotor pitch applied for the fuselage to maintain a steady heading. The revo mix increases the tail rotor pitch as the collective pitch is increased in order to make the helicopter climb, and decreases the tail rotor pitch as the collective pitch is decreased in order to make the helicopter descend. You may note that it is actually the collective pitch setting which is used to change the tail rotor, not the throttle setting, although both are of course controlled by the same stick.

The conventional helicopter transmitter will have either one or two rotary controls which enable you to set the maximum and minimum tail rotor pitch settings which will be achieved as the throttle stick is moved through its full range. The computer transmitter may have similar settings or it may be much more complex, with zero pitch points and more than one mixing curve.

These are the common functions which will be found on most helicopter transmitters. However, there are a considerable number of other options which are found on the computer sets, so I will run briefly through them.

Computer functions

Sub trim lets you adjust the neutral position for each of the channels and works just like a trim control. While sub trim enables you to adjust the neutral position for any channel, it does this by offsetting the servo neutral position, which also offsets the whole servo range of travel. This can result in the servo running out of available movement at one extreme of its range, so, while this function is extremely useful for fine adjustments, it is not a substitute for a correct mechanical set-up.

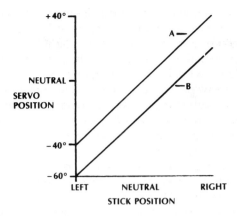

Figure 11.3 *Sub trim settings. A: 0, B: 20° left (-VE)*

Stunt trim enables you to set up the helicopter for aerobatics and to pre-select the required trim settings (for aileron, elevator and rudder) — these settings are automatically selected when the idle up (stunt) curves are selected. The trimmer control positions may then have no effect.

The **inverted flight** function is intended to make upside-down flying marginally less complicated, but in case anyone is not sure, this is not the method to use for 3-D flying. What it does is to reverse the operation of the collective, rudder and elevator channels so that the helicopter responds in the same way when inverted as it does when the right way up — for example, down elevator makes the (inverted) model dive and up elevator makes it climb. Apart from activating the switch, the only other adjustment is to the throttle stick position at which there will be no change in collective pitch when the switch is moved from one position to the other, which also sets the different collective pitch range required for inverted flight (it is advisable to ensure a sufficiency both of collective pitch range and of financial resources before attempting this exercise).

Acceleration mix is an additional torque compensation function which opposes the swing caused by changing torque values while the throttle stick is being moved. The acceleration value is programmable, but the resulting rudder response is also dependent on the rate of throttle stick movement.

If you are using a gyro with remotely controlled gain, such as the MacGregor/ JR Solid State Gyro, **gyro sense** lets you set the gain values directly between 0% and 100% and then use a switch to select them. This function may also be used to control a gyro with remotely switched gain simply by setting one value above 50% and the other below (it doesn't follow that the setting above

50% will give you the higher gain – that depends on which gyro gain pot is selected – but you must have one value above 50% and one below 50% for the switching to take place).

Programmable mixers allow mixing of any two channels with any channel as master and any channel as slave. The mixing can be permanently ON or selected in conjunction with various switch combinations. Mixing ratios up to 125% can be set, with the mixing direction reversing at the neutral position of the master channel, and the slave neutral can be offset. Mixers may have graphical displays that show the movement of the slave channel, and five point mixing curves, which means that you can set the position of the slave servo to be anywhere you want independently at each of the five points (0%, 25%, 50%, 75% and 100%) of the master channel. You can also select exponential for the curves, which rounds off the sharp corners in the curve (and alters the slave response to match!) One suggested application is to mix rudder to throttle in order to reduce the tendency to climb or descend when pirouetting with or against the torque.

There are several **failsafe** programs with MacGregor/JR transmitters, depending on the type of receiver in the model. There is no failsafe facility when using a PPM receiver. If the model is using PCM, you can choose whether you want the servos to move to pre-programmed positions (failsafe) or to remain in the last valid received positions (hold). With an SPCM receiver, all the channels may be programmed individually to hold or failsafe, whereas ZPCM only allows all the channels to be in hold or failsafe collectively.

Some MacGregor/JR transmitters may be used either as the master or the slave in the **trainer** function, and there are two modes of operation. When the **normal** trainer mode is chosen, all the channels are controlled either by the master or by the slave, depending on the position of the sprung switch on the master. However, when the **programmable function** trainer mode is in use, the control stick channels may be assigned to the slave one at a time or in any combination. A trainer lead, which is about two metres long, connects the two transmitters, via the DSC sockets, and the sprung switch on the master transmitter is held up in order to give control to the slave. Control reverts to the master as soon as this switch is released by the instructor. The pupil does nothing (except express surprise at how successfully he has recovered from the impending disaster).

There are two **timer** programs, **stopwatch** and **countdown**, either of which may be displayed on the screen while flying. The selected timer is then controlled either by the keys on the front of the transmitter, or by the sprung trainer switch (if the trainer facility is not in use). The transmitter bleeps in the countdown mode as the selected time is approached. The transmitter may also have an **integral timer** for each model, which records the accumulated time for which the transmitter is switched on with that model selected. These timers are handy for recording the amount of transmitter use between charges, if they are reset each time the transmitter is recharged. If you don't want to do a full charge every time you fly, a charge for seven times the period of use will replace the capacity used in flying. However, if the transmitter has been left unused for more than about a week, it may be safer to give a full fourteen-hour charge if you plan a long flying session.

A useful function is called simply **servo** and it shows the position of all the channels as a bar chart. There is a bar for each channel which shows the servo neutral point and the 100% and 150% travel adjust points. The servo position is shown as a cursor which moves along the bar when the control is operated. The position of the cursor represents the actual servo position, after any mixing, sub trim, travel adjust, rate settings and so on have been applied. This is a very useful function because not only does it show you just what the effect of the other functions has been but it also shows if you have demanded more servo movement than is available, which will then produce a dead band at the extreme of the control input. This can arise because travel adjust, rates, sub trim and some mixers have cumulative effects, but the servo remains limited to a maximum of 60° of movement either side of neutral.

The most advanced transmitters have functions which will only be used by the most demanding of fliers but you will find as you progress that many of them are well worth the time spent in setting them up.

Radio installation

The kit instructions will usually give some guidance on radio installation and they should be followed where possible.

You will need to operate the servos when you are connecting up the linkages, so you should plan ahead and charge both the transmitter and the receiver batteries the night before. When the radio is installed, you should always switch on the transmitter before you switch on the receiver, and switch off the receiver before you switch off the transmitter. The reason for doing this is that the servos may move all the way to their mechanical stops if there is no transmitter signal, and this can damage the linkages or the servo gears. Incidentally, the servos will not be protected by failsafe when you switch the receiver on before the transmitter because the receiver will not have stored the failsafe data if the transmitter has not been switched on. However, failsafe data is transmitted regularly whenever the transmitter is switched on and is stored by the receiver for use if the transmitted signal fails, so there is no need to switch the receiver off again if you do forget and switch it on first. I will go into greater detail when I deal with programming the failsafe in the next chapter.

Installing servos

Never install the servos without their rubber mounts but also check whether the brass ferrules, which are supplied with most servos, should be used or not – use them if there is nothing to say that you shouldn't, because they make it easier to tighten the mounting screws consistently. You should also check whether the servos are to be installed from above or below the mounts – both methods are satisfactory but installation from above is far more common. However, where the servo is shown as being installed from below the mount, it is necessary to comply with this or the linkage will not connect up correctly.

Tighten the servo mounting screws until the rubber mounts are slightly compressed, or until the ferrule is gripped – the ferrule will prevent you from over-tightening the screws. Do not compress the rubber mount too much or it will no longer protect the servo from vibration.

Installing the gyro

The model usually incorporates a flat surface for mounting the gyro and the instructions will show you where it is. Before mounting the gyro, check the

Figure 11.4 *Typical servo installation showing the servo arms cut off for clearance.*

direction of operation as described later in this chapter, because it may be necessary to mount the gyro upside down in order to achieve the correct response. The gyro may be mounted using double-sided foam tape, which you can buy from model shops or which may be included with the gyro. Clean the two surfaces with meths before applying the tape to ensure that they stick.

Installing the rest of the radio

The model usually incorporates a mount for the receiver switch, although this may need to be enlarged slightly – check what is behind the mount before cutting fresh holes. If it is difficult to reach the switch, make up a wire loop to operate it, instead of cutting a hole in the canopy. The nicad will often only fit in one place, so this should be secured before the receiver and any gyro control boxes. Make sure that the nicad cannot come loose, because if it disconnects itself, your radio controlled helicopter no longer will be. Check the centre of gravity, as explained at the end of this chapter, before finally fixing the nicad in place.

While tie wraps should be used to secure the nicad, elastic bands are sufficient for the receiver and any other light components. I use a receiver switch which has a charging flylead, so I arrange for the flylead just to be accessible when the canopy is still in place – this means that I can charge the model without removing the canopy.

When you have fixed all the various bits in place, check that all the leads are clear of moving parts and that there is no risk of a lead being pulled out of its connector. Check also that the leads are well clear of any sharp edges which might cut the insulation – file the edge or protect the lead it if necessary.

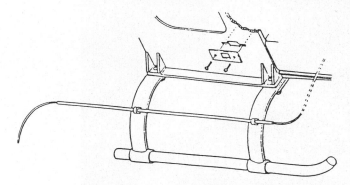

Figure 11.5 *You may need to enlarge the hole for the switch. This is how the receiver aerial should be routed.*

Never leave the receiver aerial coiled up. The aerial should leave through a rubber grommet if you want to drill a hole for it, and it should then be threaded through a plastic tube along the skids, the end being left to hang free. Don't run the aerial along the boom, the skid, or any other metal (or carbon fibre) surface. The aerial should be secured somewhere along its length so that any pull on it does not result in it being pulled out of the receiver – an easy way to achieve this is to thread the aerial through a button (or the cut-off arm of a servo output device) just before the aerial passes through a grommet to leave the canopy.

Connecting the linkages

The linkages should be made up accurately according to the quoted lengths – use the length of rod as instructed because there will only be the right number of each length. There may also be different lengths of plastic ball ends, so these should also be used as instructed.

The instructions will usually give some idea of the size and type of servo output device (disc, arm or whatever) and the distance of the hole or ball from the centre. These dimensions are not too critical and you do not need to drill extra holes in the discs – just use the nearest one to the quoted distance, moving out rather than in. When all the servos are in position and the output devices are fitted, switch the radio on and move the controls through their full ranges of travel, checking that the output devices do not clash. It may be necessary to cut off the spare arms or the unused area of a disc.

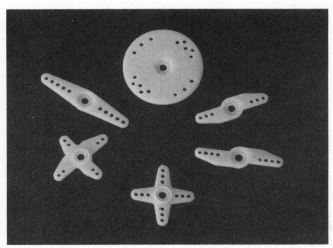

Figure 11.6 *A selection of servo output devices.*

When you move the throttle arm on the carburettor, the power output from the engine does not bear a linear relationship to the throttle position – half throttle will give much nearer to two-thirds power. To compensate for this, you should arrange the mechanical linkage from the servo to the throttle so that the throttle opens slowly at first, as the throttle servo is moved. This is achieved by positioning the output arm appropriately on the servo. You should also make sure that the throttle servo moves the throttle from fully closed (with the stick and the trimmer fully back) to fully open (stick fully forward, trimmer as required), without stalling the servo at either end of its travel – this is achieved by adjusting the length of the servo output arm and the length of the throttle linkage.

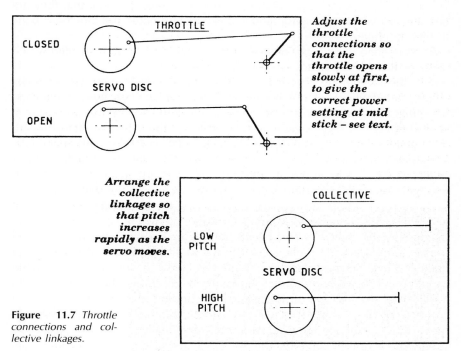

Figure 11.7 *Throttle connections and collective linkages.*

Similarly, the collective servo linkage should be arranged so that the collective pitch increases rapidly as the collective servo moves.

You should also check that the collective linkage and its geometry are set up according to the manufacturer's recommendations and that the servo is not stalled at either extreme of its travel.

The cyclic (elevator and aileron) and rudder linkages should be connected according to the instructions. If you use clevises or Z-bends to connect the controls to the servo outputs, keep the holes in the discs or arms to the minimum size to reduce the amount of slop in the controls. When you have connected the rudder servo, try holding the tail blade holder and then operating the rudder stick – if the long snake, which operates the tail pitch change, bows outwards away from the boom, use plastic tape to secure it to the boom in a couple of places.

Checking the controls and using servo reverse

When you have connected all the controls, you should check that they are operating in the correct sense (and this is why you noted the direction of the throttle operation).

If you need to reverse any of the channels and you have a transmitter which uses small sliding switches for this, make sure that the switches are securely over to the appropriate side. Some of those switches have an unmarked (and, I suspect, unintended) 'off' position in the middle, which stops the channel working altogether. Furthermore, when you send the transmitter back because it isn't working, it also gives the resident humorist in the radio's servicing department a golden opportunity at your expense, both figuratively and financially!

Operate the throttle stick and check that the throttle arm moves in the correct direction. As you move the throttle stick forwards, the leading edge of both the main rotor blades should move upwards, increasing the collective pitch.

The cyclic controls are checked by watching the swashplate from the tail end of the model looking forwards. The swashplate will pivot about its mounting on the main shaft when the cyclic controls are operated. It should be level in both axes when the cyclic stick is in the middle and both trimmers are at neutral. Move the aileron stick to the right and the right side of the swashplate should move down (with the left side coming up). Move the aileron stick to the left and the left side of the swashplate should move down.

Now push the elevator stick forwards and the front of the swashplate should move down. Pull the elevator stick back and the back of the swashplate should move down. I find that the directions of both these swashplate movements are instinctive and that this check is easy to remember.

The rudder is a bit more tricky. If you turn the tail rotor round until the blades are vertical, one blade will point forwards and the other will point backwards. Assuming that the servo direction is correct, when you move the rudder stick, the trailing edge of the blade which points backwards will move in the direction in which the helicopter will turn. If you move the stick to the right, the trailing edge will move to the right and the nose of the helicopter will turn to the right. The other way of looking at this is to regard the blade which faces forwards as though it was the rudder of a boat, not forgetting that it will move the tail of the helicopter in the opposite direction to the nose and the direction in which the nose moves is what we are referring to as the direction of the turn (stick to the right, right turn – nose moves right, tail moves left).

Setting up the gyro

The types of gyro

The simplest type of gyro has a lead to which you connect the rudder servo and another lead which plugs into the rudder socket on the receiver. The gyro has a small rotary pot, which is used for adjusting the gain, and reversing the gyro sense is achieved by mounting it upside down.

A more versatile type has a third lead which is plugged into a spare switched channel on the receiver (the gear channel is a likely candidate). It also has a separate small control box with two rotary pots, both of which can be used to set gain values – the switch on the spare channel is then used to select between them.

The ultimate development in gyros has the gain controlled directly from the transmitter. Adjusting this type of gyro is beyond the scope of this book and you should refer to the instructions which came with the radio and the gyro.

Setting the gain

If there is only one gain pot, set it to about 75% – there should be a scale round the pot to show which end is high and which is low.

If there are two gain pots, you will need to establish which switch position selects which pot. First, set one pot to 100% and the other to 0%, then turn the helicopter. If you watch the rudder servo, it will either twitch violently or not at all and this will tell you which pot is selected – change the switch position on the transmitter, turn the helicopter again and the opposite should happen. You can now set the pot which you want to use for test flying to 75% and set the other one to 25%.

Checking the sense

When you have checked the rudder direction, you should check the gyro sense. The best way of checking the gyro is to watch the rudder servo, not the tail blades. The purpose of the gyro is to oppose any turn of the model, so if the model turns left, the gyro should apply right rudder. Look at the rudder servo, apply right rudder and note which way the servo turns. With the gyro running, move the nose of the helicopter to the left (it will be easier to move the tail to the right to achieve this but don't confuse yourself in the process) and check which way the rudder servo is moved by the gyro (if the rudder servo does not move, check the gain setting for the gyro). If the gyro applies right rudder, offer up thanks, if it doesn't, find the instructions for reversing the gyro sense – *don't reverse the servo*. You may be able to move a small switch on the gyro or its control box, in order to reverse the sense, or you may have to remove the gyro and mount it upside down (which has the same effect). When you have reversed the sense, check the rudder channel again and then check the gyro sense again.

Checking the servo travel and controls

If you have installed the servos and linkages as given in the instructions, the control movements should be satisfactory, but it is still a good idea to check. Pull the throttle stick right back, then move the cyclic stick into all four corners in turn and check that the controls, pushrods and levers, particularly those in the mixing on the mast, are not binding at any time. Next, push the throttle stick fully forward and repeat the check. If there is any interference, find the cause and use the travel adjust facility to reduce the amount of servo move-ment – if the problem is one of the cyclic channels (aileron or elevator), don't forget to reduce the servo movement in both directions (or use dual rates). If the problem is serious or you are using a transmitter without travel adjust or rates, you will need to change the servo output device to bring the link nearer to the centre.

The centre of gravity

Before you finally secure the nicad and the receiver, you should check the position of the centre of gravity of the helicopter.

The centre of gravity should be at the main shaft. If it isn't, the helicopter will be trying to lean in one direction and the controls will then be offset to prevent it. The result will be a small and continually changing main blade pitch setting resulting from the elevator input and this can produce a marked vibration in the hover. I must admit that I am not sure why this seems to happen but I have experienced it and I can assure you that it does.

The best way to check the centre of gravity is to use something like a large screwdriver or an old main shaft. Remove the main blades to simplify the exercise, don't forget to fit the canopy, and leave the fuel tank empty. Now put the screwdriver across the model under the bottom of the main shaft and try to lift up the helicopter. With a bit of practice, you will eventually find the point of balance and you will be able to see if the centre of gravity is in the right place. If it isn't, move the nicad and receiver until you have corrected it, or add weight if necessary. If it is difficult to get the centre of gravity accurately under the main shaft, slightly nose-heavy is acceptable, slightly tail-heavy is not.

If the bottom of the main shaft is inaccessible, you can suspend the model by the flybar and check that the main shaft is vertical − checking that the skids are horizontal only works if the skids are at 90° to the main shaft.

Your helicopter should now be ready for its maiden flight and any further adjustments to the linkages and radio will be done when it has been flown. However, particularly for the sort of flying which you will be doing at first, the helicopter manufacturer's basic mechanical set-up will probably be satisfactory.

CHAPTER 12

Setting up the model

What you are trying to achieve, why, and how to do it, including adjusting the gyro

This chapter starts by explaining how the helicopter should respond when you operate the various controls. It continues with how to adjust it, mechanically and electronically, so that it does.

The model can only be accurately set up by being test flown and I realise that you will probably have to ask someone else to do this. However, I have included this chapter at this point because you will soon be setting up your own models and you may find this helpful as a reference.

There are two distinct parts to test flying the model. The first is the mechanical adjustment of the control linkages so that the model flies with the main rotor at the correct speed in the hover, with all the control sticks in the middle and the trimmers at neutral. The second is the adjustment of both the mechanics and the radio so that the model is in trim anywhere between a power-off descent and a full power climb. First the mechanics, second the electronics, never the other way round – the adjustments on the radio are not there to sort out a badly adjusted model. Test flying isn't as difficult as it sounds, because if you have followed the instructions with regard to the lengths of the linkages, it is likely that the model will fly reasonably well from the beginning.

Clockwise or anti, + or –, left or right (and why the skids aren't level)

This refers to the direction of rotation of the main rotor. The main rotor turns either clockwise or anti-clockwise, when viewed from above. While I have never seen this written down, within my experience if the main rotor of your helicopter turns **clockwise** when viewed from above, you should set the radio for **right-hand** rotation (and vice versa) – this setting is what controls the direction of torque compensation. Clockwise is right-hand rotation and anti-clockwise is left-hand rotation, but your transmitter may well refer to the directions as ' + ' and ' – ' so please check carefully which the manufacturer is calling positive and which negative. When you have decided which choice is appropriate, this is the first item to be set on the transmitter. Getting it wrong is not as spectacular as having the gyro working in the wrong direction but it can be more fun, since it may not manifest itself until you apply full power.

You will probably notice that your helicopter always hovers with one skid low when flown on a calm day and you may wonder why. The tail rotor is the culprit, because not only does the thrust from the tail rotor prevent the model from pirouetting, it also tries to push the whole machine sideways and the main rotor has to be inclined in order to oppose this – since the fuselage is attached to the main rotor, it, in turn, acquires a lean (which is most obvious when looking at the skids). The direction of this lean will depend on the direction of the tail rotor thrust, which in turn depends on the direction in which the main rotor turns. When I first flew a left-handed rotor helicopter, I realised that I had become very accustomed to seeing this lean always in the same direction (because I had always flown right-handed machines) and I felt somewhat uneasy until I became used to the different attitude. It doesn't bother me now so perhaps I associate the direction of lean with the outline of the particular model. Incidentally, some model helicopters seem to have a much more marked lean than others, for no obvious reason.

What you are trying to achieve and why

One of the aspects of setting up radio controlled helicopters that seems to cause more confusion than most is the relationship between main rotor speed and control response, and the way in which you should go about achieving the desired result.

The dynamics, and the aerodynamics, of a helicopter rotor head would make the subject of an entire book – in fact I have just such a book, written by two Polish gentlemen, and from about page ten onwards there is more mathematics than text (or maybe they've written it in Polish, it's difficult to be sure). I have no intention of going into competition, even if I could. The aerodynamics of the model are built in by the designer but there are a few areas in which you can have some influence.

Control response – fixed wing versus helicopter.

There is a fundamental difference between the controls of a fixed-wing aircraft and those of a helicopter. If you stall the wing on a fixed-wing aircraft, the nose will drop and the aircraft will accelerate and, assuming that you push the elevator control forward, you will regain control (which was never entirely lost). The main blades on a helicopter serve as both wings and control surfaces. They provide the lift which supports the machine and, by varying the lift as the blades rotate, they also provide the means of control. If you slow the main rotor blades of a helicopter to the point where they stall, the helicopter will fall in any attitude it chooses, the cyclic controls will have no effect whatsoever and control is now entirely lost. Unless you can unstall the main rotor blades and thereby regain control, gravity is unlikely to be distracted from its sole purpose in life. What usually happens is that the helicopter falls vertically, thereby reversing the normal direction of airflow through the rotor disc. This increases the drag on the main blades to such an extent that they either swing back in their blade holders and wrap themselves round the main shaft or the engine is simply unable to produce sufficient power to accelerate them – the difference is academic from a financial point of view.

The effect of rotor speed on control response

The control response of a fixed-wing aeroplane becomes more sensitive as the airspeed increases, and high-performance aircraft have various devices to prevent the pilot from damaging the machine by over-controlling at high speed. The control response of a helicopter varies with the main rotor speed in the same way, although the effect is complicated by the changing gyroscopic forces (control response does also vary with airspeed, but to a lesser extent). It is, however, true to say that the control response becomes more sensitive as the main rotor speed is increased.

The difference between fixed-wing aircraft and helicopters is that the control response of the fixed-wing machine is a function of its speed through the air (and is therefore easy for the pilot to anticipate), whereas the helicopter can have varying control responses without ever leaving the hover. If you use a computer transmitter, it is quite possible to set a model helicopter up in the hover so that the collective pitch is reduced as the throttle is opened further – the model will not climb even though the engine is producing more power and the main rotor is turning ever faster. The control response will change with the rotor speed, but the model need never leave the spot (although it will definitely become harder to keep it there!).

The ideal control response

The aim is to set the model up so that the rotor speed does not change during the flight, and this will ensure that the control response is also constant.

Incidentally, if you have watched competitions which involve both hovering and aerobatic manoeuvres, you may have noticed that the main rotor speed increases noticeably as the competitor leaves the hovering area and commences the aerobatics. The increase in rotor speed is because he has changed to a different throttle pitch selection, with a higher main rotor speed, in order to increase the control response for the aerobatics. This is achieved by using a transmitter which has a switch which selects one of several throttle pitch relationships. These allow different main rotor speeds to be used for different manoeuvres, thereby changing the control response. What you should also note is that the main rotor speed does **not** change **during** either the hovering manoeuvres or the aerobatics.

It is also worth remembering that the speeds of the tail rotor and the main rotor are directly linked. It is not unknown for a novice to set his model up so that the collective pitch is far too high, which means that the model lifts off with the normal amount of torque but with a very low main rotor speed. This results in the tail rotor speed being so low that it cannot produce enough thrust to oppose the torque, and the model will now turn in the opposite direction to the main rotor, even with full opposing tail rotor (rudder) applied. In fact, this is the symptom which is usually described.

So what we want to achieve is a constant rotor rpm from lift-off throughout the flight to touchdown. How do we go about it? The starting point is the hover.

The main rotor speed

As I have said before and will probably say again, if you are new to helicopters, there is a Catch-22 – if it isn't set up, it won't fly, but if you can't fly it, you can't set it up – so you do need help.

The first thing you need to know is the correct rotor speed for the hover. There are specialist helicopter tachometers available for measuring the main rotor rpm and they can be helpful. If you have access to one, it is not necessary to hover the model over it. If you open the throttle until the model is light on its skids, you will be able to note the rotor speed, and what the model sounds like at that speed, and the rotor speed should not increase by much, if at all, for the subsequent lift off. If your handbook does not quote a rotor speed (or you have lost it), between 1,400 rpm and 1,500 rpm will be satisfactory for small machines (in the .30 cu.in. range) and less for larger ones. I know of people who are flying models with main rotor speeds below 1,000 rpm, but I would suggest no less than 1,300 rpm until you are a competent flier and are sure of the effect of any changes and the problems associated with low rotor speeds.

Transmitter control positions for the hover

The throttle stick must be in the mid position when the helicopter is in the hover, in order that the various trimmers and compensation functions can work correctly. The **hover throttle** and **hover pitch** control trimmers (if fitted) are only effective when the control stick is close to its mid position, and, if differing torque compensation settings (revo mix) are available, they will change over at the mid-stick position.

The model should be mechanically adjusted to be in trim in the hover and the gyro should be switched off to check the tail. The throttle should be central and all the specialist helicopter trimmers (**hover pitch, hover throttle** and **collective pitch trim**) should be in their mid positions. High and low collective trimmers have no effect on the collective pitch when the control stick is in the mid position, but, if they are fitted, it is good practice to check their positions – again, mid settings allow for adjustment in either direction if necessary.

Mechanical adjustment

The starting point

All the pitch and throttle facilities should be set to standard values. Use the **reset** function on a computer set (but check the servo directions and operation afterwards). Servo travel should be set to 100 per cent, unless you have used small adjustments to prevent the controls from binding or the servos from stalling. Torque compensation should be set to zero. The mechanical set up on the model should be according to the manufacturer's recommendations or, in their absence, as discussed in the previous chapter.

Test flying the model – the first lift off . . .

When you are happy with the mechanical set-up, you are ready to fly the model. You can have the gyro switched on for the time being but . . .

The gyro is used to detect unwanted swings of the tail and to produce a signal which will oppose them. If, however, you fit the gyro the wrong way up in the model, or you have its reversing switch in the wrong position, the gyro will detect the swing and produce a signal to the servo which will *increase* the rate of rotation instead of opposing it. This can be extremely spectacular but usually not for long enough for many people to have the chance to admire your skill – if I have just installed the gyro or have tinkered with it, I always open the throttle *very slowly* for the first flight.

... and the hover

The worst problem will occur if the collective pitch setting is too high and the model lifts off with very low rotor speed with a strong wind blowing – you may find that you have insufficient cyclic (elevator) control to stop the model from pitching nose-up and coming backwards to bite you. I strongly recommend that you avoid flying in strong winds unless you are very sure of the model and you are a competent flier. If the model shows any signs of lifting off with very low rotor speed, close the throttle immediately.

Open the throttle very slowly and note the engine noise. If this becomes excessive and the model does not lift off, close the throttle again, stop the engine, and alter the length of the appropriate pushrods to increase the pitch settings of both the main blades. In the absence of any guidance, the pushrods to alter are the ones nearest in the linkage sequence to the blade holders – adjust them by equal amounts, taking into account whether the ball joints are reversible or can only be fitted in one direction. If the model lifts off at low rotor speed, adjust the same pushrods but in the opposite direction, so as to decrease the pitch of the main blades.

When you have managed to persuade the helicopter to hover, check the blade tracking. Hover the helicopter with the main rotor disc at eye level and note whether both the blades follow the same track through the air. If they don't, the different coloured tracking tape which you fitted will enable you to identify the high and low blades. If the tracking is out and the main rotor speed is low, reduce the pitch of the high rotor blade, and vice versa. When the tracking is correct, adjust both blades together until the main rotor speed is as required, decreasing the pitch if the rotor speed is low and increasing it if the speed is high.

Now check the position of the throttle stick when the helicopter is in the hover. If the stick is below the mid-point, you need to reduce the amount of throttle opening. This is done mechanically by delaying the rate of throttle opening, which is achieved by removing the output device from the servo and turning it one spline in the closed direction. You will now have to adjust the length of the throttle pushrod, check the closed and full throttle positions, and, possibly, adjust the length of the servo output arm.

If the stick is above the mid-point, you need to increase the amount of throttle opening. This is done mechanically by increasing the rate of throttle opening, which is achieved by removing the output device from the servo and turning it one spline in the open direction. As above, you will now have to adjust the length of the throttle pushrod, check the closed and full throttle positions, and, possibly, adjust the length of the servo output arm. If this does not make sense, please read the section on *Connecting the linkages* in the previous chapter for an explanation of the relative positions of the throttle and collective servo arms.

You will now have the helicopter hovering with the throttle stick in the mid position, but the main rotor speed may require further adjustment by changing the pitch of the blades (and this may again mean that the throttle has to be further adjusted). Each adjustment you make to the pitch and throttle mechanics should be smaller and you will soon be able to estimate what the necessary changes should be.

When the collective and throttle are adjusted correctly, you should also make any necessary changes to the elevator, aileron and rudder linkages so that the helicopter hovers hands-off (which is a relative term where helicopters are concerned, but there should be no tendency always to drift in one particular direction when the sticks are released).

You will now have a helicopter which hovers with the throttle stick in the middle and with the main rotor running at the correct speed. What comes next?

Climb and descent

The final objective of all this tinkering is to have a helicopter which climbs, descends and hovers with no change of rotor speed, thereby maintaining a constant control response (I find that it also tends to confuse any watching fixed-wing pilots, who assume that models should rev up to climb or go faster). You have the desired rotor speed in the hover, so now slowly open the throttle fully and check that the model climbs away with no change in rotor speed. You have already checked visually that the throttle servo is moving the throttle from fully closed to fully open, so the only adjustment which should now be necessary is to the collective. If the main rotor speed increases as the throttle is opened, you need to use more collective pitch (and vice versa), but remember that the hover setting is correct so you do not want to disturb that. However, if you keep the collective pushrod in the same relative position in the hover but increase the size of the servo output device, you will apply more collective pitch at full throttle (and less at closed throttle). A bit of experimentation with drilling holes in output discs at different radii should enable you to achieve the desired effect, and you will have a machine which hovers and then climbs away without a perceptible change in the engine note. Climb the model to a generous height and close the throttle slowly and completely – if the rotor speed now drops and the model seems to be defying gravity (briefly, anyway), you need less pitch (more negative) at the closed throttle position but, unfortunately, this can only be achieved by disturbing the climb and/or hover settings so this is where you go and buy a helicopter transmitter.

If, however, you now have a helicopter which flies superbly, you will be wondering just why you spent all that money on a computer radio when you don't need to use it.

Unfortunately (or fortunately, if you happen to manufacture computer radios) no mechanical set-up can ever be that good and, furthermore, there are lots of other advantages to specialist helicopter sets as you will see.

Using the transmitter functions

The figures which follow are correct for MacGregor/JR radios. Other makes may not be identical, but the basic principles will still be correct and the figures will be similar. Please refer to the handbook for your radio if you have any problems.

All the above description refers to making mechanical adjustments to the model and this should be the first method for setting up the helicopter. Indeed, if you are using a basic four-channel transmitter, this will be the only method available to you.

Computer radios have a wide variety of functions which can be used to make your helicopter behave exactly as you would wish. Unfortunately, these various functions do affect one another, so some understanding is useful of each individual function and how it does what it does.

Travel adjust

You should always adjust the helicopter mechanically so that it hovers with the sticks in the middle and the correct rotor speed. However, if you have a transmitter with servo travel adjustment, you can use small amounts to achieve precisely the right degrees of throttle and collective control movement − if you need more than about 20%, you should change the servo output device to a longer or shorter one.

Travel adjust is a function which enables you to alter the amount of servo movement separately for either side of neutral. At 100% the servo will move through a total arc of 80°, this being 40° either side of neutral. You can increase the servo travel on either side of neutral separately by up to 50%, which gives a total arc of 120° − if, however, you increase only one side by 50%, the servo will move through a total arc of 100° but that will NOT be 50° on either side of neutral, it will be 60° on one side and 40° on the other and the servo neutral position will be unchanged. This is particularly relevant

movement than you need is that you can always restrict this movement by using the collective pitch curve but if you subsequently need it as the engine runs in and develops more power, you will not disturb the other settings by having to change the travel adjust again.

A small tip which I find useful if you are using a computer set is to increase the throttle setting for the 25% stick position – it prevents the head from slowing down on descents where you are not closing the throttle completely and you will find it produces a much smoother response (and less of a violent swing of the tail) if you open the throttle a bit too quickly.

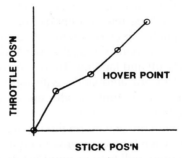

Figure 12.3 *Try increasing the 25% stick setting for a smoother response from low power descents.*

You should now have a helicopter which climbs, descends and hovers with no noticeable change in rotor speed. I hope you think that it was worth all the effort. Of course, when you open the throttle (with no gyro) the tail swings violently in one direction and when you close it, it swings violently in the other but adjusting the torque compensation to stop this is the next item on the list.

Revolution and acceleration mixing

When the engine turns the main rotor, the torque reaction tries to turn the fuselage in the opposite direction and, at any particular power setting, you will need a corresponding amount of tail rotor pitch in order to prevent the fuselage from turning. Obviously, you could apply rudder to achieve this, but revolution mixing will do it for you. I believe that many club fliers don't understand revo mixing and use the gyro to do the job. However, the result is that the gyro gain has to be set higher than otherwise necessary and this restricts the power of the tail rotor too much.

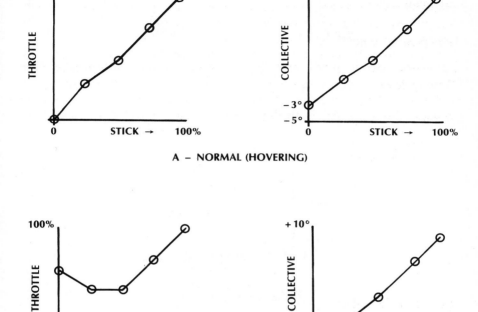

A – NORMAL (HOVERING)

B – AEROBATICS

Figure 12.4 *The throttle and collective curves for aerobatics give higher head speed and more negative pitch.*

The torque reaction needs to be divided into two components, the first being the constant value which applies when the throttle is at a particular setting and the second being the changing value produced by acceleration or deceleration. The revo (revolution) setting compensates for the first component and the acc (acceleration) setting compensates for the second. The interesting point to note at this juncture is that if you have set the model up so that the head runs at a constant speed throughout, there should be *no* acceleration or deceleration phase so you don't need any acc compensation. This does seem to be the case and I never bother to set this mixing – the gyro will cope with any transitional changes anyway, without the gain being set any higher than normal.

Which way round?

If you didn't set the direction of rotation of the main rotor, now is the time to do it.

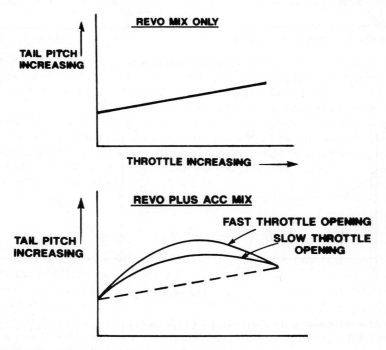

Figure 12.5 *Revo mix and revo plus acc mix.*

Setting the revo mix

Revo mix actually mixes the collective pitch setting, for the selected collective pitch curve, with the tail rotor pitch. This will appear as a tail rotor pitch setting which changes as the throttle stick is moved, but it is worth noting that the tail rotor pitch is related to the collective pitch at that stick position, not the throttle setting or simply the stick position itself. If you change the collective pitch curve, the revo tail pitch setting will also change, but note that this will *not* be the case if you use the travel adjust facility to alter the collective settings. The mixing is clever, but not that clever! The value which you enter in the revo mix function on a computer radio is actually a mixing ratio, which enables the computer to calculate how much tail rotor to apply for any particular setting on the collective curve. If you are using a manual transmitter, the revo settings (or setting, if you only have one adjustment) are still mixing ratios but the collective curve is either a straight line (or, if you prefer it, a curve of infinite radius), or two straight lines which meet at the hover point.

Setting the acc mix

Not all transmitters have acceleration mixing but the principle behind it is of some interest and you may wish to experiment. Some transmitters allow you to set the direction for the compensation independently from the revo mix, others assume that you will use the same direction.

What you are setting in this function is an amount of rudder correction and you may be able to set both the extent of the rudder movement and the duration. However, as with revo mixing, you are actually setting a mixing ratio and the computer will decide how much rudder to apply. This time, the deciding factor is the speed with which the throttle stick is moved – the faster the movement, the larger the compensation.

Back to the test flight again

For this exercise, you will need to switch off the gyro so I suggest that you wait for a fairly calm day – if there is a switch on your gyro, the tail servo should still work normally with the gyro switched off and there is no need to go pulling out plugs and rewiring the helicopter. The first revo adjustment to be set is the one above the hover point and for this you need to trim the rudder channel of the model in the hover as accurately as possible. Now slowly apply full power and, when the model is climbing steadily, note that you have to apply rudder to prevent the model from turning. The effect will be most marked if you climb the model with little forward speed, since this will minimise the tendency of the tail to slipstream. Now land the model and adjust the **up** revo setting – most computer radios seem to need about 25% – then repeat the climb and you should need to apply less rudder than before. Keep tweaking until the helicopter climbs on full power with no need for rudder at all – please keep an eye on the fuel level while doing this, it can be very easy to forget. Incidentally, these percentage figures are related to a main rotor speed of around 1,500 rpm – if you use less, you will need more compensation, because the torque will be about the same but the tail will be turning slower and therefore delivering less thrust.

Next comes the **down** revo setting and for this you need to descend with the throttle either closed or nearly so. I find that 30% is a good starting point here but I do still fly the model once with no down setting just to confirm the extent of the swing.

If you have an acc mix on your transmitter, this can now be set. Again, you start with the model in the hover but this time you open the throttle somewhat more briskly and note the initial swing, if any. Now land the model and adjust the acc value (or values), then fly the model again. Keep tweaking until there is no swing when the throttle is opened, then climb the model to a safe height and close the throttle fairly quickly. There should be no swing now either, but, if there is, you will have to set a compromise acc value, since there is only one adjustment.

That's all there is to revo and acc mixing. It's free, it's there to help and it really is worth the effort of setting it up. It does take the load off the gyro too, which means you can turn the gain down and have a more manoeuvrable helicopter.

Setting the gyro gain

When you are adjusting the gyro, it may help to have a basic understanding of what the gyro is doing and why.

Gyro response with varying gain

The correcting signal which the gyro sends to the tail servo is the product of the **error** signal which is detected by the gyro sensor multiplied by the **gain** setting. So what does the gain control actually do? If the gain is set to zero (note; the minimum gain on some gyros is about 20%), the gyro will do nothing. The gyro will still detect the rotation of the model but the electronics will not send any correcting signal to the tail servo (error signal × 0 = 0). If the gain is set to 100%, the maximum correcting signal will be sent to the servo, but the actual value of the correcting signal will always depend on the size of the error signal.

Gyro response to tail inputs

When you hover the model and then put in rudder in order to make the model pirouette, the rudder signal is passed through the gyro unchanged and the model starts to yaw. However, the gyro does not know why the machine is yawing, so it now tries to stop it. The yaw rate will be reduced by the gyro but this will then mean that the correcting signal from the gyro is reduced and the yaw rate will increase again. What happens in practice is that a state of equilibrium is reached very quickly and the model achieves a constant yaw rate. It is worth noting that if the yaw rate is slowed, as by a cross-wind, the gyro will reduce its correction, allowing more tail pitch displacement and thereby tending to stabilise the yaw rate. The reverse process will apply if the yaw rate is speeded up.

Gyro limitations

The gyro will respond to increasing yaw rates of the model until the moving element reaches the limit of its travel and hits the stop. This situation is unlikely to be reached in normal flight but may be seen during aerobatic manoeuvres such as stall turns and pirouettes. This will produce a curious effect if a low gain setting is being used. Consider the case of a model which is pirouetting; as the rudder input is increased, so the model rotates faster and the gyro correction increases, moderating the servo movement but still allowing an increasing rate of rotation. However, eventually the gyro reaches its mechanical limit and its maximum correction is being produced – if more rudder input is now applied, there will be no further increase in compensating correction from the gyro and the rudder will appear to have become more effective. This will not occur at high gain settings because the rotation rate of the model will be restricted to the point where the gyro does not reach its mechanical limits. The solid state gyros are quoted as having much higher operating ranges and should not experience this phenomenon, even at low gain settings. Aerodynamic considerations should ensure that the rotation rate of the model remains within the capability of the gyro.

Setting the gain

The simplest way to set the gain is to wind it up until the tail starts to wag and then turn it down until it just stops. When you are first learning to fly, this is probably the best setting. At the 75% figure, which I suggested you set to start with, the tail will probably wag so you will need to turn the gain down slightly. If the tail still wags, you will need to have another look at the tail pitch control mechanism to make sure that there is no slop or lost motion under load – these are the commonest causes of tail oscillation.

When you start to fly the helicopter around, you may find that the tail wags when the machine is in fast forward flight – this is where the dual gain gyros are useful because you can now use the switch to select the other gain setting. As you become more experienced, you should experiment with lower gain settings because they do make the helicopter much more responsive.

Finally, setting the failsafe

There is a lot of argument and misunderstanding about failsafe and its function in life. Failsafe is designed to protect the rest of the world *not* the model and this is particularly true of helicopters.

When you program the failsafe servo positions into the transmitter, they are stored there and, whenever the transmitter is switched on, they are transmitted periodically with no action being required on your part. When the receiver is switched on, it receives the failsafe data and stores it *while it is switched on* – the data is lost as soon as the receiver is switched off. The receiver now looks at the incoming transmission and accepts the signals as long as they comply with certain built-in parameters but, as soon as they fail to comply (or just fail), the receiver ignores them and either holds the servos or moves them to their pre-programmed failsafe positions. However, the receiver continues to monitor the incoming transmission and, as soon as the signals again comply, the receiver returns to normal operation.

You cannot switch failsafe off. What you can do is to choose what you want the servos to do when the transmission fails, the alternatives being **hold** or **failsafe**. If you choose hold, the receiver will simply keep the servos in the positions in which they were when it last received a valid signal. If you choose failsafe, the receiver will move the servos to the positions which you have programmed into the transmitter.

The purpose of failsafe is to prevent an uncontrolled model from flying off and crashing some distance away, perhaps in the middle of a town. Failsafe should ensure that the model crashes nearby but you can at least ensure that it doesn't do so on full power. Unfortunately, with a helicopter the difference is academic but having the throttle closed may prevent the model from thrashing itself to bits on the ground.

If you choose hold and the signal is lost with the model on full power, it will crash with full power applied, unless the signal is regained. If you choose failsafe and program the throttle to close, a loss of signal could result in the model hitting the ground slightly earlier than it would have if you had chosen hold (or half throttle), which allows less time for the signal to be regained. What you do with the cyclic controls and the rudder is anybody's guess, but I would program the collective to follow the throttle – if you close the throttle, reduce the collective pitch to minimum or you could find that the rotor head had stopped turning and the situation was irrecoverable even though the signal returned before the model hit the ground.

If pressed, I would suggest choosing failsafe with the throttle closing to idle and the collective pitch reducing correspondingly. The cyclic controls and the rudder should be centred.

The helicopter will now be adjusted for basic flying and these settings will still be satisfactory for simple aerobatics.

CHAPTER 13

Before your first flight

Getting everything ready

The model is all ready to fly but there are a few things which you can do to be ready for the great day (or for any subsequent one). If you are using a training undercarriage, it should be fitted and secured in place.

Battery charging

You will have used your radio equipment while setting up the model and so you should be quite familiar with it. You know how to charge it, but you may be wondering how often you should charge it and for how long.

The optimum charging rate is called the 'ten-hour rate' and this is calculated by dividing the nicad capacity by ten (i.e. 50 mA for a 500 mAh nicad pack). However, assuming that you are charging at the ten-hour rate, you should charge the pack for 14 hours from fully discharged because there is an inefficiency in the charging, and this time should be increased to 16 hours for a new nicad pack. The useful thing about this charging rate is that it will cause no damage if the time is exceeded (even by several hundred per cent) and this means that you can safely charge the nicad pack for 14 hours, even when it is not fully discharged.

Most helicopter radio sets have a 600 mAh transmitter pack and a higher capacity receiver pack, which is typically 1,200 mAh. The combined charger for these sets will have outputs at 60 mA for the transmitter and 120 mA for the receiver, which means that 14 hours will charge both from fully discharged.

If you are using a standard (50 mA) charger to charge a larger-capacity nicad pack, you will need to increase the charge time. Divide the charge rate into the nicad capacity and multiply the result by 1.4 to establish the full charge time (for a 1,200 mAh pack this gives 24 × 1.4 = 33.6 hours).

All the previous discussion refers to fully-discharged nicads, but what about the pack which you only used for ten minutes the previous weekend or the one you charged but didn't use at all? The difficulty here is that nicad packs do discharge when not being used, but they do it at their own particular rate, which can vary enormously. If you only fly at weekends, you can safely charge the nicads for 14 hours before each flying session, or for seven hours if you charged them the previous weekend but didn't fly (assuming that you are using the appropriate charger).

The other difficult problem is deciding for how long you can safely fly before the nicads will be discharged. The transmitter is straightforward, it should last at least two and a half hours if the nicads are in good condition and fully charged (and it has a battery indicator to tell you when it is getting low). You can easily check how long your transmitter batteries will last by charging them fully and then leaving the transmitter switched on at home – you must fully extend the aerial for this check to be accurate, since the transmitter will use less power with the aerial retracted. The receiver nicad is more difficult because the current consumption of the servos will vary considerably depending on several factors. If the control linkages are stiff, you are using five high-powered servos and a solid-state gyro (which increases the rudder servo activity), doing aerobatics, and the outside air temperature is freezing (which reduces the nicad efficiency), then a 500 mAh nicad could last as little as 30 minutes (a high-power servo can draw up to five amps if it is being heavily loaded). At the other extreme, the same nicad could last 75 minutes in a well-adjusted model, flown gently on a sunny day. The first precaution you should take is to use the largest capacity nicad which is practical. Receiver nicad packs are now available in capacities ranging up to 1,700 mAh – I use the 1,000 mAh or 1,300 mAh packs which are only slightly larger than the 500 mAh versions. If you cannot use the larger capacity packs, make sure that you can change the receiver nicad reasonably easily and take a spare with you to the flying field. In practice, when you are first learning you will probably find that 45 minutes is about as long as you can manage before you start to lose concentration. If you do go in for long flying sessions, I suggest that you invest in one of the battery monitors which I described in the previous chapter.

While you are charging the radio batteries, don't forget the ones for the starter and glow plug.

Transmitter frequency control

I described the frequency allocation system in Chapter 6, *Everything you need to know about radio systems*. Most organised flying sites will use some method of frequency control to ensure that only one transmitter is in use on any particular frequency at any particular time. If you have joined a club, the club will advise you of the method in use and of any requirements (the most common is a wooden clothes peg on which you write your name and transmitter channel – this is then clipped to a board while you are flying to indicate that you are using that channel).

When you acquired your transmitter, it will have been supplied with two crystals, one of which plugs into the transmitter (Tx) and the other of which plugs into the receiver (Rx) – if they were already fitted, you should check the labels on each of them. Also included with the transmitter there should be an orange pennant and a set of numbers which correspond to the channel number of the crystal. The numbers should be stuck to the pennant and the pennant should then be attached to the transmitter aerial – this enables other modellers to check which channel you are using without having to ask you. However, this only works if you always display the correct channel number on the pennant. If you change your crystals for a pair on another frequency, make sure that you change the pennant as well.

I cannot over-stress the importance of frequency control – nothing is more disheartening than the completely unnecessary destruction of two models through lack of care or a misunderstanding.

The range check

As well as checking that the nicads are up to the job, you can also check that the transmitter is transmitting and that the receiver is receiving. This is the purpose of the range check, which should be done before each day's flying or if work has been carried out on the model or its radio system, or if any crash damage might have occurred. The range check works on the assumption that if the performance of the radio is satisfactory at fifty metres with the restricted transmitter power which is available with the aerial retracted, it will be satis-factory in flight with the normal transmitter power which is available when the aerial is extended.

All you need for a range check is an open space which will allow you to walk fifty metres (yards will do) from the model and still see that the controls are working (or, better still, signal to someone who is standing by the model and can see that **all** the controls are working).

The worst place to try to do a range check is at the flying field when other pilots are flying, for reasons which will become apparent. It is not possible to do a meaningful range check when there are other transmitters in use with their aerials fully extended.

How to carry out the check

The maximum range check should be carried out with the transmitter aerial fully retracted, ideally with two people. One should hold the model at shoulder height so that the extended receiver aerial is pointing at an angle of forty-five degrees from the vertical. The other should walk away, with the transmitter held so that the retracted aerial is in a parallel plane with the receiver aerial and also at forty-five degrees from the vertical but pointing in the opposite direction. The two aerials should form a vee when seen by a third person. If the controls on the model do not operate consistently and without interference at a distance of fifty metres or more from the transmitter, the radio system should be checked by the relevant service department.

It will now be apparent why the busy flying field is the last place to try to do a range check – apart from any other considerations, a transmitter which is switched on with the aerial extended (as will be that of anyone who is flying) is likely to cause interference to your model because of the reduced power of your transmitter with its aerial retracted (even when you are using different channels).

The range check should be done at home or at the flying field before flying starts.

Transporting the model

I will assume that you have checked that it will fit in the car, but before you do commit yourself to transporting the helicopter, it is worth considering how you are going to secure it. Surprisingly enough, it is very easy to damage a model simply by letting it fall over – a bent feathering spindle or main shaft is a common result – so you should make the necessary plans in advance. The main blades should either be removed or secured; for pod-and-boom models, you may be able to buy a foam support which clips round the tail boom and holds the blades up, taking the strain off the controls. The helicopter should be transported standing on it skids but it should be secured so that it cannot fall over or slide.

I have a purpose-made board with rails so that the model cannot slide, and clips to secure the skids so that the model cannot fall over. The board is backed with old carpet to prevent it from slipping and my pit box is used to weigh the whole thing down in the back of the car.

CHAPTER 14

The day arrives

The weather is fine, your instructor is available,
everything is ready . . .

I hope that you will have been able to arrange for someone to help you, in which case they will probably take you through what follows in their own way. However, I have written this as though you are doing it unaided.

The weather

Helicopters can be flown in most weather conditions – the main problem with rain is that it gets into the transmitter – although I would not recommend standing in the middle of a large field holding a very effective lightning conductor (the transmitter aerial) when there is a thunderstorm anywhere in the vicinity. I have flown in wind speeds exceeding thirty mph, but it isn't fun and I don't recommend it – the main problem is the turbulence.

What you need for your first flight is a clear, dry day with a steady, light (no more than 5 mph) breeze. If an experienced pilot is going to test fly your model before you fly it (which is strongly recommended), he may well be prepared to do so in conditions which are not suitable for you, but that will save time when the right weather does finally arrive. It will also give you a chance to take the model home to do any final adjustments and to check all the nuts and bolts for security. Don't be afraid to say no if you think that the conditions are not right for your first flight.

At the flying field

The helicopter should have been test-flown and adjusted by an experienced helicopter pilot and I shall assume that this has been done. If you have previously managed to find yourself a suitably qualified instructor, now is the time to hand over to him.

If this is your first visit to a club flying site since joining, introduce yourself and ask about any flying restrictions, frequency control and so on (the club should have told you the procedures which are used). Check that the club allows helicopters to be flown at the same time as fixed-wing models and also check whether there is a separate area for beginners to fly helicopters. Most clubs will have some understanding of the differing needs of helicopters and will have made suitable arrangements.

Safety checks

These fall into two groups, those which should be done before each flying session (in addition to fully charging both the transmitter and receiver batteries) and those which should be done before each flight.

Before each flying session (or if the model is damaged, tipped over, or landed hard)

1 Check the whole model for loose or missing nuts, bolts etc.
2 Check the whole model for damage or cracking, particularly the side-frames and undercarriage.
3 Check the blades for damage or loose covering material.
4 Check all the linkages for wear, loose ball-links etc.
5 Check the drive system for loose belts or gears and for wear in the gears.
6 Check the radio system for loose servos, unsecured leads or components, and for damage to the aerial.
7 Check the fuel system for split fuel tubing, loose tank or fuel filter.

Before each flight

1 Before starting, check the positions of all the controls, trimmers and switches.
2 Switch on the transmitter, then the receiver, then operate the radio controls and check for full and free movement, with no slowing of servo operation.
3 Check that the receiver aerial is clear of moving parts.
4 Start the model and carry it to the flying area.
5 Check the controls at high rotor rpm, just before lift-off.
6 If there is excessive vibration, stop the engine and investigate.

Engine starting

When you have sorted out the flying arrangements, you are ready to begin, and the first thing to do is to fill the fuel tank. If the engine is new, do not alter

turn right. Spend some time doing this until you are accustomed to the feel of the controls, then gradually open the throttle until the model becomes light on the undercarriage and can be skidded across the ground. If you become confused, slowly close the throttle, relax, then start again. Remember periodically to check the amount of fuel remaining in the tank, although no harm will come to the model if it does run out of fuel while it is on the ground (as the fuel runs out the engine will accelerate briefly before it finally stops – keep the throttle closed and wait, the model will not take off because there is no positive collective pitch being applied when the throttle stick is fully back).

The way to learn to fly a helicopter without damaging it is to take everything very slowly. What you are eventually aiming to achieve is a stable hover at a height of about half a metre but at first you will be sliding the model about on the ground, using progressively more throttle to make the model lighter until you are achieving short hops with the model completely airborne (at this stage don't try to reach half a metre, keep the model just clear of the ground). Aim to keep the model in the same place by correcting its tendency to drift off – don't just close the throttle the moment the model starts to move in any direction (if it moves left, apply right aileron and if it moves backwards, apply down elevator, and so on). If the model climbs higher than you want it to, don't slam the throttle shut, just pull it gradually back until the model is descending, then close it completely when the model is on the ground. Always position yourself about three metres directly behind the model for each fresh attempt – don't be tempted to open the throttle when the model is at an angle to you or is some way off or is not on level ground.

You may notice that the model seems to move in the same direction every time you lift it off – this is normal and you should not try to adjust the trim controls to compensate for it (I am assuming that the model has been correctly set up and that the trims are set for a stable hover). Always try to handle the controls gently and smoothly, particularly the throttle. If you slam the throttle shut, the model will hit the ground hard with negative pitch on the main blades and with the rotor head slowing down. These are the ideal conditions for the main blades to hit the tail boom. If you touch down with some power still applied and some positive pitch, the main blades will be held out by centrifugal force and the chances of a boom strike are minimal. If the model has been correctly set up, it will descend whenever the throttle stick is below the mid position – there is no need to pull it right back.

You will probably find that you begin to over-control after a while (even more than you did to start with!) and this is the time for a break. Do not be tempted to keep going, the mental effort required at first is very high and half-an-hour will probably be more than enough for one day.

After the flight

When you finally decide that you have had enough for the day, pull the throttle trim back to stop the engine, switch off the receiver then the transmitter, then carry the model and transmitter back to the starting area. Next you should return the frequency peg (or comply with whatever system is in operation for frequency control at the flying site). You should now pump any remaining fuel out of the tank in the model, both to reduce the risk of spillage and to prevent the volatile components from evaporating and leaving a residue of oil behind which will cause future running problems. The helicopter should be cleaned of exhaust residue, mud, dead insects and so on before being securely stowed in your transport. Since nearly all helicopters drip oil from the exhaust, it is worth taking some precaution to avoid this problem.

When you reach home

Don't just park the helicopter in the workshop until the next flying session. Finish cleaning the model if you didn't do it at the flying field. Next, go over the model thoroughly, checking for loose nuts and bolts and making sure that nothing is coming adrift − silencers have a habit of working loose and should be sealed with silicone, which can also be used as a thread lock. Check the gyro mounting and any securing straps for the receiver nicad and check that the radio leads are still held clear of the moving parts.

If you have needed to apply trim to any of the controls, now is the time to carry out any mechanical adjustments and to centre the trimmers − it is good practice always to adjust the model as soon as possible, so that you don't have to remember where the trimmers should be before each flying session.

CHAPTER 15

Hovering, circuits and simple aerobatics

Basic flying techniques – what comes next

I would like to start off with a couple of definitions.

Airspeed: this is the speed which the aeroplane is doing through the air. It takes no account of any wind which is blowing (in fact, the aeroplane doesn't actually know that there is a wind blowing). It is the speed which you would see on the airspeed indicator of a full-size aeroplane.

Groundspeed: this is the speed which the aeroplane is doing over the ground. It is the speed which the aeroplane will appear to you to be doing if you are standing on the ground, and it will only be the same as the airspeed if there is no headwind or tailwind. However, the model is rarely flying exactly either upwind or downwind and, furthermore, the wind at several hundred feet will not be blowing in the same direction or at the same speed as it is at ground level. These factors combine to make groundspeed an unreliable indicator of airspeed, especially when allied to the helicopter's well-known ability to fly sideways.

So **groundspeed** is what you *think* the aircraft is doing whereas **airspeed** is what the aeroplane *knows* it is doing.

This brings us to a couple of maxims which should be engraved on every pilot's pit box.

Aeroplanes fly on airspeed, not groundspeed and *When flying downwind, if the groundspeed equals the windspeed, the airspeed equals zero.*

There is no trick to learning to fly radio controlled helicopters, it seems to be simply a question of practice and more practice. I never teach a student any of the fixed-wing techniques, like 'when the model is coming towards you, you prop the down-going wing up with the control stick'. How do you decide at what point the model is coming towards you, as opposed to flying past you?

I believe that the art of flying helicopters lies in recognising the different attitudes and then responding to them instinctively, because the inherent lack of stability means that you just don't have time to think what to do next. The other problem is that helicopters are basically unforgiving and there is often only one way out of a situation, where a fixed-wing model might have given you a choice.

The usual escape route from a difficult situation is to apply full power and climb away. This will be completely unnatural if you have a fixed-wing background and you will have to persuade yourself not to close the throttle. Unfortunately, this escape route is not available to the novice until he has mastered flying the model around and returning to the hover, which is why I advise you to keep the model below one metre to start with.

Mastering the hover

Over one spot

Always start with the model facing into wind and facing away from you. As you become more confident, you will be able to hold the model in the air for longer but you should still confine yourself to keeping the model facing away from you and to no more than one metre above the ground. When you can keep the model more or less in one place, you should start to move it around deliberately, noting the different attitudes and the way the rotor disc tilts as you apply cyclic inputs. You will discover that you can apply down elevator and the model will accelerate forwards, not downwards. Up elevator will make the model move backwards, and you should take care not to land it either when it is moving backwards or when it is in a tail-down attitude, because either of these will increase the risk of a boom strike.

When you are happy with the model facing away from you, try using the rudder to turn the model so that you can practise hovering with it facing left and right. Don't try to hover with the nose facing you yet.

Tail-in hovering circles

This is an exercise which will improve your co-ordination. At first, it should only be tried when the wind is calm or nearly so. With the model in the hover facing away from you, apply aileron so that the model moves sideways but keep the model moving so that it describes a complete circle around you, always facing away from you. You will need to apply rudder to keep the model facing away from you and you will also need a small amount of up elevator to keep the model tracking in a circle. You can fly this manoeuvre slowly at first, then speed it up as you become more confident. Don't always turn in the same direction but alternate, so that you become used to both left-and right-hand circles.

When flown in a wind of any strength, the hovering circle becomes a good test of co-ordination, with continually changing control inputs being required as the model progresses from a head wind, through a cross wind from one side, a tail wind, a cross wind from the other side and back to a head wind again.

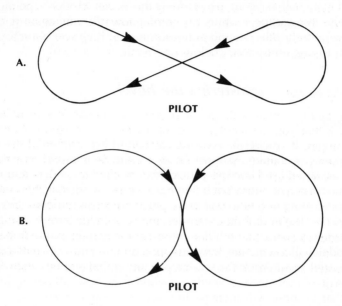

Figure 15.1 *Figure eights: start with A, progress to B and you have mastered flying towards yourself.*

Moving the model around

When you can hover the model with a fair amount of confidence, stand facing into the wind as usual and try flying a slow figure eight from left to right and back again in front of you. Make the turns, at either end of the figure eight, away from you (and into wind) and, at first, fly the straight legs in front of you so that the model is only tracking slightly towards you. At first, you may find that the model is always pointing into wind but gradually you will learn to use the rudder to keep the model pointing in the direction in which it is travelling.

If you gradually widen the turns so that the model is tracking more towards you as it goes across in front of you and you continue to do this, eventually you will be flying straight towards yourself. Throughout this exercise, you should have an escape route planned, which should involve turning the model whichever way you prefer until it is facing away from you.

At first, this manoeuvre should be flown slowly but you can gradually speed it up if you feel confident, practising bringing the model back into the hover at regular intervals.

Now, still flying figure eights, try climbing the model while it is going away from you then descending it while it is coming towards you, again returning to the hover periodically. Once you have mastered this, you have acquired all the skills necessary for flying circuits.

Checking the model

Before you go any further, I suggest that you ask an experienced helicopter flier to check that your helicopter is set up correctly throughout its throttle/collective ranges. If you have confined yourself to hovering (and the motor was new when you started) the model may need to be adjusted now that the engine has loosened up. The model should be checked in a full power climb, to ensure that the maximum pitch setting is correct and that the engine is neither overspeeding (too little collective pitch) nor slowing down (too much collective pitch). The model should be descended with the throttle completely closed in order to check that the rate of descent is correct and that the main rotor is not slowing down. The torque compensation on the transmitter should also be adjusted to minimise the tail rotor inputs which will be required with power changes.

Flying a circuit

This is the time to remind yourself of the two maxims I quoted at the beginning of this chapter – *aeroplanes fly on airspeed, not groundspeed* and *when flying downwind, if the groundspeed equals the windspeed, the airspeed equals zero.*

Furthermore, when flying downwind, if the groundspeed is less then the windspeed, the model is actually **flying** backwards, which is quite possible with a helicopter, as you have already discovered. Quite apart from the fact that this will make controlling the machine difficult, there is a strong possibility that it may turn round and then be **travelling** backwards (although now **flying** forwards) which will leave you totally confused. There are two precautions which you should take when learning to fly the model around. The first is never to fly in a strong wind and the second is never to try to hover the

manoeuvre for when you become disorientated and just keep practising until you become familiar with the attitudes, and the control responses become instinctive. Eventually you will be able to land and take-off with the helicopter facing you just as easily as when it is the other way round.

Pirouettes

I don't want to give away the secret but pirouettes are easy – all you need to do is to start with the helicopter in the hover and level, then apply rudder to make the fuselage rotate. The action of applying rudder will not significantly disturb the helicopter's attitude and the fuselage will now simply spin round the mast. At first, you will find that the helicopter will gradually drift off and you will have to centre the rudder and bring it back. However, eventually you will find that you can leave the rudder applied and fly the helicopter while it is rotating. The trick is to leave the rudder alone and just concentrate on the cyclic controls while watching the rotor disc – remember, the helicopter will only go where the disc is pointing. When you have mastered pirouettes, try a pirouetting circle.

Loops

The loop is flown in a similar way to flying a fixed-wing model. Select idle up, then, with the helicopter flying fast and level in a straight line, gently pull up elevator and, as the model passes the vertical, reduce the throttle setting to about half. Keep the elevator applied as the model goes inverted and when it reaches the vertical going downwards, start to apply throttle again. The first time will probably be a mess, but you should be able to adjust the application of elevator and collective until the result is tidy. As you experiment, you may find that need to close the throttle fully when the model is inverted at the top of the loop, which will apply negative lift and will keep the loop from tightening up. You should have no problems but, if the model is reluctant to finish the loop, keep full up elevator applied and open the throttle to maintain the rotor speed.

Rolls

The roll is achieved by flying the model fast and level, then applying full aileron and holding it until the model is level again. Don't use up elevator as you would with a fixed-wing model because you will lose too much speed when the model is inverted but do enter the roll with the model level and travelling as fast as possible. As you experiment, you will find that you need a small amount of negative lift at the inverted stage but beware of using too much or of letting the rotor speed slow down.

If the model is reluctant to roll, either apply opposite aileron and abandon the roll or keep going until the model is inverted, then centre the aileron and apply up elevator to pull through half a loop.

Stall turns

The entry is the same as for a loop, again using idle up. However, as soon as the model is pointing vertically upwards, centre the elevator and pull the throttle stick back to just below the mid position, then apply full rudder to rotate the model through 180°. Briefly allow the model to dive vertically then recover in the same way as you pull out of a loop, applying throttle and elevator so that the model finishes at the same height as it entered the manoeuvre but going in the opposite direction.

Too much gyro gain may make the model reluctant to rotate but you should have enough gain for the model to stop rotating when you centre the rudder for the brief dive.

The 540° stall turn simply involves leaving the rudder applied while the model rotates one and a half times, instead of just a half.

Autorotations

Contrary to popular theory, helicopters do not crash as soon as the engine stops. I have been asked to test some dreadful helicopter engines over the years (none of which are on the market now!) and a knowledge of how to carry out a successful autorotation has saved the model many times.

For practising autorotations, you will need to have the throttle hold facility set so that the engine continues to run at a reliable idle speed when throttle hold is selected. The collective pitch should be set so that you have 3° to 5° of negative pitch on the main blades when the throttle stick is pulled right back – the only way to decide if you have enough is to close the throttle fully and see how the helicopter descends. The rate of descent depends on several factors and the minimum collective pitch can really only be set with experience but the one vital element is that the main rotor speed must not drop in the descent.

Starting with the model downwind at about 100 feet and flying into wind, you should practise closing the throttle fully and then carrying out a power-off descent at about 45° so that the model would arrive at a point just in front of you at a height of about three feet. At this stage, don't select throttle hold, just practise the descent and then apply power to climb away. When you are confident of arriving at this spot, position the model as usual, close the throttle and select throttle hold. Fly the descent as before but as the model reaches about three feet, start to apply up elevator to stop the model moving forwards and to reduce the rate of descent. As the model reaches about a foot off the ground, start opening the throttle (only the collective pitch will change because you have selected throttle hold) and gradually lower the model to the ground. The rotor speed will reduce as you apply collective pitch but there should be plenty of time to land the model.

This all sounds very easy but it does take a lot of practice. I have found out the hard way that you can successfully change your mind and switch throttle hold out, so that you can open the throttle and start again, but once the model is below about twenty feet, it is usually better to continue the autorotation. Trying to operate the switch and fly the model at the same time usually results in the model still hitting the ground but now with full power applied.

This is not intended to be a comprehensive guide to helicopter aerobatics – a whole book could be written covering little else – but it will give you some basic ideas on which to build. The secret, as always is to take it slowly and keep on practising.

CHAPTER 16

Routine maintenance

*Don't just put it away, look after it and it will reward you
(with a few tips on troubleshooting on the flying field)*

Helicopters are unlike fixed-wing models in that it is necessary to carry out some routine maintenance after every day's flying (you should do the same with fixed-wing models but very few pilots seem to bother). You will usually find that there is little to do but it is always worth checking to make sure that nothing has come loose or started to wear. It is far better to do this after the last flight of the day than just before going flying next time, because if you do find anything which needs to be changed, you won't be wasting flying time while you are changing it.

After the last flight

At the first opportunity you should drain the fuel tank and clean the model – methylated spirits will remove the exhaust residue. If you find that the oily residue is black, look for a loose screw or bolt which retains something like an aluminium tail brace (the black colour is caused by the aluminium being chafed).

Draining the fuel tank serves two purposes. It prevents the methanol from evaporating in the tank and leaving just the oil and it also provides a useful check on the plumbing to ensure that all the fuel is available when flying the model. Obviously, this means that you must drain the tank by using your fuel pump in reverse to suck the fuel out through the line which goes to the carburettor. This should be disconnected from the filter on the tank side – never drain the tank by sucking the fuel through the filter because this will mean that any dirt will be trapped by the filter and may subsequently affect the running of the engine. If there is any dirt in the tank, this will be returned to your fuel container but will subsequently be trapped by the filter in the refuelling line. You could, of course, fit another filter in the line which returns the fuel to the container but I have never bothered.

If you cannot suck all the fuel out of the tank, it is a sure sign that something is wrong with the pick-up inside the tank. The tube to the clunk weight may have come adrift or split, or the clunk weight itself may have come off the tube or got jammed in a corner of the tank. Whatever it is that is wrong, it needs to be rectified and you may need to change the length of the tube to the clunk in order to prevent it from happening again. There used to be a popular theory that silicone tubing grew when continually in contact with fuel, and this resulted in the clunk eventually touching the side of the tank. It doesn't matter what the cause may be, if you are having trouble with the engine running oddly for no obvious reason, or if the engine will not empty the tank before it runs out of fuel, check that all is still well with the plumbing inside the tank and replace the clunk tube if necessary.

This is also the opportunity to inspect all the fuel lines to ensure that there are no splits developing and that nothing shows any signs of chafing or coming off. It is worth checking the filter every few flights to make sure that dirt is not building up and that any seal fitted in the filter is still serviceable. If you have noticed any fuel drips when the helicopter is in the hover, now is the time to investigate thoroughly for small splits in the tubing. These are most common where the tubing slides over one of the nipples, often the one on the carburettor. The sharp edge round the nipple prevents the fuel tubing from slipping off but it can also cut the tubing if it is too sharp or if the tubing is pulled at an angle to the nipple. The other common cause of leaks in flight (when the fuel tank is under pressure from the exhaust muffler) is that the filter seal has failed or that the filter halves are not screwed tightly together. If you have a problem with the filter coming unscrewed, slide a short length of large bore silicone tubing over it. This has the added bonus of preventing the metal filter housing from vibrating against any nearby metal part of the helicopter and generating metal to metal noise, which can be a cause of radio interference.

What to look for

You should check the whole helicopter for loose (or missing) nuts, bolts and screws every time you put it away, not forgetting the muffler bolts and the bolts which hold the engine mount in the frames.

Check for wear in the control linkages, particularly if the swashplate uses plastic moulded balls. Operating the controls while watching the servos will show up any slop in the servo bearings and also any serious friction in the controls – you will see the servo moving in its mount as it fights with the controls. If you do see the servo moving, remove the control linkage from the servo output disc and then move the controls by hand – this will tell you what sort of load is being put on the servo. Check also that the servo mounts are secure.

Inspect the receiver aerial for cuts or damage and also check that the servo leads are remaining clear of any moving parts. Losing two or three inches off the end of a JR receiver aerial will make no difference whatsoever to its range, but I can't speak for other makes.

If your helicopter uses a belt drive tail, look at the front of the tail boom for white dust – this is a sign of wear in the belt and you should immediately check the plastic gears and the belt tension to see if the belt is rubbing anywhere. A damaged tail belt should be replaced immediately. The correct manoeuvre or, more accurately, the only manoeuvre, which will allow you to recover from a broken tail belt, is a climbing pirouette (because you have no tail drive) followed by an autorotation. This does take practice and the model will be drifting with the wind during the climb – I speak from experience.

Vibration

Vibration is a killer. It destroys models and radios faster than anything else and should never be ignored.

Troubleshooting on the field

I assume that your model didn't vibrate when it was last flown, so what we are looking at here is a vibration which has developed with no obvious cause.

The first point to consider is whether you have changed anything. Simply moving the nicad, or changing it for one of a different weight, may be enough to start the model vibrating, if the change has moved the centre of gravity away from the main shaft.

If the vibration has developed suddenly and you have changed nothing, the chances are that something is loose or bent. If the main blade tracking is also out, that will produce vibration but you should investigate to find out why the tracking has gone out. Make sure that a ball-link hasn't been pushed on too far so that it is loose on the inner side of the ball and check that the bolts which act as pivots for the various mixing levers are secure and tight enough.

If you have removed the main blades since the last flight, check that the blades have been refitted in the original holders and not swapped over. Make sure that the blade bolts are equally tight and that the blades can swing equally freely (with the helicopter held with the main shaft and main blades horizontal, the blades should just swing down under their own weight). Next, and I know that it sounds ridiculous but I have seen it done – you haven't fitted the main blades backwards, have you?

If the helicopter falls over on its side, perhaps in the car on the way to the flying field, this can be enough to bend either the feathering spindle or the main shaft. You should check the main and tail blades for damage or for missing trim or balancing tape. Out of track main blades will produce vibration anyway, but you will need to investigate why they have gone out of track. If the blades can be tracked but the tracking keeps changing, the feathering spindle is probably bent.

If you can't find any explanation and you are satisfied that there is no damage, try altering the collective pitch in the hover so that the rotor speed is lower (or higher, but try lower first). This may cure the problem – some helicopters seem to have a particular rotor speed at which they vibrate. Don't worry about the shudder which most helicopters go through as you accelerate the engine and rotor head to flying speed – providing, of course, that it stops before flying speed is reached. Try lining up the main blades before opening the throttle. This will reduce the out-of-balance forces until the blades align under centrifugal loads.

If the tail suddenly develops an erratic hunting, check that the gyro is still securely mounted.

Persistent problems

Assuming that nothing is bent or damaged, it can be worth re-checking the balance of the main blades if they are wooden. Wood does dry out or absorb moisture and it is possible that the blades have become unbalanced for this reason.

If the tail vibrates and a boom stay is an option, try fitting one, in order to reduce the flexibility of the tail end. Check the balance of the tail blades.

Turn the main gear slowly to check that the mesh is constant throughout the rotation. If there is a high spot on the gear or it is warped or the teeth are damaged, change it.

If there is a high frequency vibration or the fuel foams in the tank, use a dial gauge to check the clutch and flywheel alignment.

Finally, if all else fails, try swapping components to discover which is causing the problem.

Radio problems

If you have noticed any twitching of the controls, particularly when the engine is running, shut down immediately and look for any loose nuts, bolts or screws. If two metal components touch and vibrate together, they will produce static electricity which will cause the servos to twitch (called 'glitching'). Switching on the radio and touching the boom or the engine mount with a screwdriver will often produce this effect if you are using a PPM receiver and you may also notice it when you connect the power supply to the glow plug.

Helicopters are generally very reliable providing they are correctly assembled in the first place. In fact, one of the problems is that they will often carry on for months with absolutely no work being necessary and this can lull you into a false sense of security. It's worth developing the habit of doing a regular check whenever you put the model away.

CHAPTER 17

After a crash

So you've bent it – what to look for and how to fix the sort of problems that arise when you run out of ideas just before the model runs out of height

It's often said that nothing looks so pathetic as a dead helicopter – well it's often said by my fellow club members anyway. Actually, the truth can be very different and a model which looks distinctly terminal may well be airborne again surprisingly quickly (but, unfortunately, rarely surprisingly cheaply).

You can also take the opportunity to fit upgrade parts. For instance, if you keep finding that the fins are cracked, you might want to fit carbon fibre ones. If you do consider replacing the manufacturer's components with alternatives, make sure that the quality is as good as, or better than, the originals and, if the replacements are cheap, ask why. As a general rule, you can always fit a manufacturer's upgrade parts to his machine although you should check that you can fit just the parts you require – it may be necessary to change other components as well. I would have no worries about replacing non-mechanical parts like undercarriages, fins or canopies with ones from another source, but I would be very wary about using components like masts or feathering spindles from alternative sources, unless I was able to check the materials and the accuracy of the machining. Never replace cap head bolts with pan heads, because cap heads are supposed to be stronger (never, ever, use anything but cap head bolts for the main blades). If possible, buy replacement bits like nuts and bolts from an engineering supplier (where they will be considerably cheaper and of at least as high a quality as the originals).

So what are the common types of damage and what should you look for?

Main rotor blade contact

Rotor blades: if the main rotor blades contact anything while under power, stop as soon as possible and check for damage. If the blades are covered with heatshrink or adhesive covering, this may hide serious damage and it should be removed for checking (make a note of any balancing and tracking tape and replace it with the same amount when you have checked the blade). Bend the blade into a curve and check that it **does** form a curve and not two straight lines with a sharp angle where it has cracked across the width. Composite (glassfibre or carbon) blades must be checked to ensure that the leading or trailing edges have not split open – running them in this state could allow the weight to escape with potentially disastrous results. Please, never try to repair composite blades, it is too dangerous. The balsa trailing section of wooden blades can sustain minor damage but the hardwood leading section is highly stressed and any damage must mean that you scrap the blade. You should make sure that the blade weights, if fitted, have not been damaged or loosened and you should also inspect the blade mounting holes and the bolts for any signs of damage.

Feathering spindle: this may be bent. On a model which has a one-piece spindle, like the Hirobo Shuttle or the TSK My Star 30, remove one main blade and use a box spanner or nut runner to rotate the spindle – if it is bent, the blade holder(s) will wag up and down as you turn the spindle. Another clue is a model whose main blades keep going out of track, particularly when you have done aerobatics or power-off descents where the throttle was closed very fast – the negative loading makes a bent spindle revolve in the dampers and this puts the tracking out.

Main shaft: vibration is usually the clue to a bent main shaft, if it isn't obvious. You can remove the main blades, then spin the shaft by the flybar and look for a wobble on the head. If you try this with the main blades still fitted, they will never remain in a straight line, which means that the whole assembly will be out of balance and will wobble anyway. I invested in a dial gauge for checking that flywheels and clutches were installed square and the addition of a pair of vee blocks means that I can check main shafts as well, when they have been removed from the helicopter.

Main blade pitch arms: if the blades are out of track immediately following the incident, a bent pitch arm is often the cause. You can adjust the blades back into track but the results depend on the type of bend in the arm. If the arm is bent outwards, the amount of pitch change being applied at maximum and minimum stick positions will have been reduced even though the hover setting is correct and this will result in out of track running at high and low power. Unfortunately, you will now have a model which runs smoothly in the hover but vibrates when you can't see it closely, that is when you are flying it around. This doesn't really matter when you are still learning and are only hovering the machine but beware of the potential problems as you progress to circuits.

Blade holders: these are so tough nowadays that they are usually the last parts to sustain damage, but they are very highly stressed in flight so do check them regularly, particularly around the bolt holes. With the types which consist of upper and lower halves, I have heard stories of the halves separating under really severe loads, so it is worth checking that all the screws are still in place and tight. While you are checking the holders, inspect the bolts which retain the main blades and make sure that the nyloc nuts are still locking sufficiently.

Control linkages: blade impacts cause some highly unpredictable loads on the linkages and you should check all the ball-links to make sure that none of them have been stretched or split. I have seen a ball-link where the plastic ring had split completely through and the split wasn't visible unless you looked very closely. Needless to say, it would have failed as soon as any load was put on it.

Tail boom strike

This is usually done with the main blades so all the above comments will apply.

Tail boom: small dents are acceptable but you should check that the boom is still absolutely straight and that any dent is not large enough to cause interference with the tail drive belt or wire. Check also that the dent has not moved or loosened a tail drive wire support.

Tail drive belt: if the boom is bent sufficiently for it to have trapped the belt, particularly while sufficient power was applied for the tail rotor to be being driven, the belt should be replaced. It won't fail immediately but will wait until you are in no position to carry out the required pirouetting climb and autorotation which is the only escape from a tail drive failure at low altitude. Beware of the appearance of white dust in the area of the tail belt – this can mean that the belt is not running correctly somewhere out of sight and is rubbing against something.

Tail gearbox: the shock from a severe boom strike (where the blade hits the side of the boom rather than just bouncing off the top) can result in damage to the casing of the tail gear box. Check closely to be sure that no bits have fallen off and that the casing is not split and is still clamped securely to the end of the boom. If the gearbox is of the enclosed type, it is worth separating the two halves to check that there is no damage to the plastic gears or the idler pulley.

Tail end damage

If this is caused by a tail-down or backwards arrival, the previous comments will also apply.

Vertical tail fin: damage is usually obvious and confined to the fin itself. If serious, check the mountings to the boom and tail gearbox. If there is no other damage, the model can be hovered with the lower half of the fin missing but there is less protection for the tail blades.

Horizontal tail fin: again, damage is usually obvious but check that the boom stays (if fitted) are not damaged at the ends. If you are fed up with replacing cracked fins which seem to split for no reason, check for vibration and fit carbon fibre replacements, which are available from the main blade manufacturers. They cost a bit more than the standard units but will soon pay for themselves.

Boom stays: these are quite soft and can often be straightened if bent. If you have a model where the stays are secured with self-tapping screws which tend to work loose, consider replacing the screws with nyloc nuts and bolts.

Tail blades: the standard plastic ones put up with an amazing amount of abuse but beware of running them when they are out of balance due to missing bits. Carbon fibre blades develop frayed (and very sharp) ends which can be carefully trimmed if necessary.

Tail blade holders: most likely candidates for damage are the various bits of the control linkages, particularly the lugs on the blade holders. Do check for damage because the previous comments about tail belt failure and pirouetting climbs apply equally to any tail control failure.

Main structure damage

If the model hits the ground level and with the main rotor being driven fast (or stopped), you may find that the model appears to be undamaged, or to have sustained only a broken undercarriage. This can be a tricky situation because you do really need to check the model thoroughly before flying it again.

When the sideframes stop moving, the head assembly tries to continue on downwards and the bearings on the mainshaft will be the first items to take the load. This can often result in the bearing support moulding in the sideframes being broken, which means replacing the sideframes. If you suffer a heavy landing, try to visualise which parts will have been stressed and look first for damage in those areas.

The nicad is another solid mass that will try to continue on its merry way and it may well damage the servo frames and radio section in the process. Make sure that all the servos are where they should be and that all the screws which hold them are still in place.

If an undercarriage cross member is broken but the skids are intact, you may be able to replace the cross members on their own without having to buy skids as well – ask your local model shop.

Radio check

Following any heavy arrival, you should *always* check the radio equipment. If the model is still flyable, at least carry out a visual check to make sure that nothing has come loose and no plugs have come undone, then do a range check, before flying it again. A more thorough check should include all the wiring and connectors for any signs of cuts or damage and a check on all the cases for cracks or broken lugs. Check for damage to the aerial, both externally and where it is soldered to the circuit board inside the receiver case – beware of any sign of damage because the wire may have broken inside the insulation. With modern JR receivers, the loss of two or three inches from the end of the receiver aerial will still leave you with adequate range, particularly for flying helicopters, but I cannot speak for other makes. If the case shows any sign of impact, have the receiver checked for internal damage by the manufacturer's service department. The inside of the receiver crystal is actually fairly delicate but cannot be checked, so it would be wise to scrap the crystal if its case is damaged. Again, the service department will be able to offer advice.

Nicads are fairly tough but it may be worth removing the heatshrink covering if you are in any doubt, to check that the wiring is still secure.

If the model is severely damaged and you are doing a major rebuild, it is worth taking the radio switch to pieces and checking inside for oil, dirt or corrosion. At the same time, you can inspect the switch wiring for wear or damage.

In conclusion

I don't know what the best approach is when you have bent your favourite machine. Some people say that you should immediately start to take it to bits, others say that a decent mourning period is more appropriate. Personally, I like to start work on the repairs as soon as possible, at least to the extent of stripping and cleaning the bits and trying to assess which parts will need to be bought. At the very minimum you should disconnect the receiver nicad and drain any fuel from the system – don't forget that the silencer will have a quantity of exhaust residue inside it which will be looking for a new home, and your car seat or carpets will do nicely.

Just how far you will need to strip the model after a crash depends on several factors. I am writing this during August and everything outside is dry and dusty – every day is the hottest day since at least the day before, and a crash under these conditions would probably involve a total strip down just to get rid of all the dust. On the other hand, in winter you might have far less to do in order to clean off the model and the softer ground might well have resulted in less damage from the impact. Incidentally, if you do decide to do a major rebuild, washing all the bits (preferably except the radio) in hot soapy water is a cheap and effective way of removing the filth. If there is any chance that grit or dirt has been sucked into the carburettor intake, you will need to strip the motor – don't, under any circumstances, turn the motor over if it might have ingested anything, because you may be grinding whatever it is into the piston or the bearings.

Whether you decide just to do a quick clean up or to start the rebuild immediately, don't despair. Even if the bill looks like being horrendous, there will be a lot of undamaged parts and the rebuild will very rarely approach the cost of a new machine. I actually enjoy building model helicopters, even if I don't enjoy having to pay for the experience.

Scale models

Kit, conversion or scratch-built

The first radio controlled helicopters to appear were all scale models and this added to their designers' problems, because of the poor power-to-weight ratio and the difficulty of changing components. However, manufacturers soon came up with the pod and boom configuration which now dominates the market.

Kits

There are two usual approaches to kits for scale machines. You will have noted several photographs of the Hirobo Lama in the book, and this is a typical scale kit. The kit is complete and is assembled in the same way as a pod and boom

Figure 18.1 *The author with a Morley Jet Ranger.*

machine, with spares being available as usual. Many of the components are shared with the Hirobo Shuttle but the sideframes and layout of the mechanics are completely different, and the Lama uses a wire tail drive instead of a belt.

The other alternative is to buy the mechanics from a manufacturer and then fit one of his (or possible someone else's) fuselages to it. While you will be buying two packages, they will have been designed to fit together.

Conversions

The starting point for a conversion is a pod and boom machine. You then buy a bare fuselage and you do the necessary modifications to make the fuselage fit, although most fuselages will use a similar method of attachment. The fuselage manufacturer will advise you which pod and boom machines are suitable.

A major consideration here is whether the pod and boom machine uses a belt tail drive or a wire one, bearing in mind that one cannot normally be converted to the other. It is very difficult to change the length of a belt drive tail because there are very few different lengths of belt on the market. A wire drive, on the other hand, can be cut to almost any length. Another consideration is whether the tail boom is straight, which is essential for a belt drive, whereas a flexible wire drive will tolerate a shallow curve.

Figure 18.2 *The Lama flying level – fast!*

Figure 18.3 *This is a Jet Ranger fuselage fitted to a Hirobo Shuttle.*

You may be able to find some decals to suit the model but most scale fliers use an air brush to produce a painted scale finish.

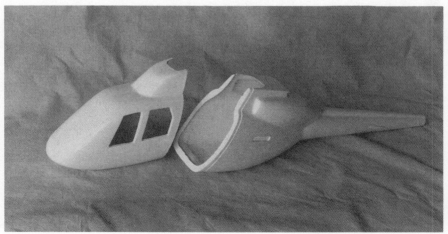

Figure 18.4 *This is how the Squirrel fuselage looks before any work is done.*

Scratch-built

Modellers who build helicopters from scratch usually start with a commercial set of mechanics but do everything else themselves, including making the fuselage. The only comment I can make is that they have my utmost admiration and I wish I could do it too.

Scale helicopters have not enjoyed much popularity for some years – the last scale competition to be held at the British Nationals was some years ago – but the recent appearance of some complete kits for .30 machines is a welcome trend.

CHAPTER 19

Conclusions

I hope that you have found this book interesting and useful and that, if you were undecided, you will now join the world of rotary flight.

The challenges are endless and there is always something new to try. When you have mastered a sequence forwards, you can always try it backwards. I have not mentioned 3D flying, with its flips, sideways loops, backwards rolling circles and any other manoeuvre that you can conceive (and some that you can't!). But don't go to a model flying display and come away with the impression that 3D is the ultimate challenge for every helicopter flier – there are many of us who have no ambition even to fly a helicopter upside down. One of the best display pilots around is always remembered for the way his flying resembled full size.